Rabbit

Rabbit

Victoria Dickenson

REAKTION BOOKS

To Thumper, the first of her tribe to share our home

Published by
REAKTION BOOKS LTD
33 Great Sutton Street
London EC1V 0DX, UK
www.reaktionbooks.co.uk

First published 2014

Printed and bound in China by C&C Offset Printing Co., Ltd

A catalogue record for this book is available from the British Library

ISBN 978 1 78023 181 5

Contents

1 A Natural History

The rabbit is a paradoxical beast. It is an animal at once both pet and supper, pest and product, invasive yet endangered, prolific yet declining. Even its natural history displays a strange contradiction, a story of an animal both wild and feral, with a worldwide distribution made possible by the actions of its greatest predator.

'WHAT, IF ANYTHING, IS A RABBIT?'

Rabbits are lagomorphs, along with pikas and hares. The word lagomorph derives from the Greek and means 'hare shaped'. It would seem evident that everyone knows what a rabbit is, but it has been less obvious to biologists and particularly to evolutionary palaeontologists, for whom rabbits have long presented a puzzle. In 1957, Albert E. Wood, a vertebrate palaeontologist specializing in rodents, asked 'What, if Anything, is a Rabbit?'[1] His answer was not a rodent, but not an antelope either. Until 1912 biologists since Linnaeus had grouped rabbits with rats and mice, based on their gnawing and constantly growing incisors. Closer examination of their teeth (vertebrate palaeontologists are as obsessed by teeth as dentists) revealed a distinctive difference between the dental patterns of the lagomorphs and rodents, and it appeared that there were 'no good reasons for continuing

Oryctolagus cuniculus, the European rabbit.

Nuralagus rex, the giant Minorcan rabbit. Reconstruction with a living European rabbit, Oryctolagus cuniculus, in the foreground for comparison.

the association of these two great groups of mammals'. However, were they more closely related to the bounding antelope and leaping deer, as suggested by the author of a paper of 1912 that separated them from the gnawing rats and scurrying mice?[2]

Lagomorphs today are once again grouped with rodents, but not as closely as they once were. With Rodentia, Lagomorpha form one part of the Glires, a large mammalian grouping called a clade, which in turn is part of a larger dynasty termed a 'crown clade'. There are four such dynasties of living mammal, each descended from a common ancestor in the remote past. Not surprisingly for those who love rabbits, primates are also members of the great dynasty that includes the lagomorphs, making our disturbing sense of familiarity with them more plausible. While they may be grouped together as Glires, rodents and rabbits split apart an unimaginably long time ago, when dinosaurs still walked the earth. A recognizable lagomorph (with distinctive teeth and very long feet) hopped through what is now Mongolia some 55 million years ago, and 10 million years later the lagomorphs had spread throughout Eurasia and North America. The modern families of the order Lagomorpha, comprising the Ochotonidae (pikas) and Leporidae (rabbits and hares), probably originated in Asia, though there is evidence to suggest that the Leporidae were native to North America. Whatever their origin, today's lagomorphs are found on all continents with the exception of Antarctica.

Even as eminent a scientist as Albert Wood suggested that 'bunny' would be the best common name for all the lagomorphs, since the term 'rabbit' is also often used to refer to the hare. Rabbits and hares differ somewhat in their appearance, hares being longer and more angular, but they are distinguished chiefly by their reproductive traits. Baby rabbits are born naked and helpless, with their eyes closed and requiring a mother's care. Baby hares or leverets are born ready to run, fully furred, with wide-open eyes.

Within the family of the Leporidae, there are 32 or so different species in the hare genus *Lepus*, and about 26 species in the ten genera of rabbit. North and South America, Africa and Asia boast three genera each, whose names all include the Latin root *-lagus* for 'rabbit' or 'hare'. In the western hemisphere, the largest and most widely known genus is *Sylvilagus*, which includes the cottontails and tapeti (marsh and swamp rabbits and the little-known tapeti rabbits of South America), as well as the *Romerolagus* or volcano rabbit of Mexico, and the *Brachylagus*, or pygmy rabbit, the smallest of the rabbits, found in the Great Basin and mountains of the United States where the sagebrush grows. There are also three distinct genera in Africa: *Poelagus*, or the Bunyoro rabbit of

Central Africa; *Bunolagus,* the long-eared, critically endangered riverine rabbit of South Africa; and *Pronolagus,* or reddish rock rabbit. Asia also has three distinct rabbits: *Pentalagus,* the primitive Amami rabbit of Japan's Ryukyu Archipelago; *Caprolagus* or bristly rabbit of India, Nepal and Bhutan; and the secretive striped rabbit of the tropical forests of Sumatra and Vietnam, *Nesolagus.* The tenth rabbit genus is the one whose history has been so deeply intertwined with that of its distant primate cousin *Homo sapiens.* The European rabbit, *Oryctolagus cuniculus,* was once confined to the Iberian Peninsula, southern France and a small part of northern Africa, but has become a global species whose natural history, due to human actions, is most unnatural (as is later recounted).

It seems strange that the number of species of an animal as common as the rabbit should be approximate, but scientists have recently been surprised both by the appearance of previously unknown rabbits, and by the re-evaluation of existing subspecies. In the winter of 1995–6, Rob Timmins, a British biologist, came upon three dead rabbits in a market in Laos, and recognized them at once as something quite new. Rare striped rabbits (*Nesolagus*) from Sumatra had been known from skins collected between 1880 and 1916. These freshly killed rabbits resembled the *Nesolagus* rabbit, but genetic analysis revealed they had evolved separately from them for approximately 8 million years. This newly discovered species, the Annamite rabbit, has been named *Nesolagus timminsi* after its discoverer.[3]

Among the New World cottontails, speciation and subspeciation is high, and in 1986, researchers examining the DNA of what they thought were New England cottontails living in the southern Appalachians realized that these cottontails were in fact a separate species (*S. obscurus*, the Appalachian cottontail). In 2000, biologists working on South American tapeti rabbits discovered yet another new species, the Venezuelan lowland cottontail (*S. varynaensis*), which is larger and darker than other South American cottontails, and had seemingly been hiding in plain sight among its congenors.[4] In 2007, a tapeti subspecies from Panama first identified in 1877 was deemed a full species (*S. gabbi*). As researchers examine rabbit DNA and range more widely in once-impenetrable forests in the Old and New Worlds, it is likely that the number of distinct rabbit species will grow.

THE FORM

'The lagomorphs are a rather distinctive group, and there rarely seems to be any question as to whether any given animal is or is not a lagomorph.'[5] As Albert Wood suggested, rabbits are not difficult to recognize. They are built to run. They have long legs and large hind feet, and their tibia and fibula (equivalent to the shin and calf bones in people) are fused, adding strength to their hind limbs and reducing their overall weight. Their feet are

Rabbit signs: tracks in snow.

covered with dense fur and sport strong claws. Their skulls are thin and partially fenestrated (pierced with openings in the bone) to make them lighter. They have large ears that are longer than they are wide, and tails that are small relative to body size. Long ears, a small tail, short front paws and long, powerful hind legs form their easily recognized profile. Their gait is the 'half-bound', a powerful leap with the hind feet that sends them hurtling through the air, until first one, then the other of the forefeet touch the ground, a '1-2-3' beat that Beatrix Potter, author and rabbit owner, described as 'lippity-lippity'. For many North Americans the distinctive two-and-two mark of the Eastern cottontail is the most easily identified animal track on snow-covered fields.

Rabbits run on their toes, but walk on the soles of their feet. On the run, a cottontail rabbit can attain speeds of 35 to 40 kilometres per hour in short, zigzagging leaps, some as long as 3 metres in a single bound.[6] The animals are built for quick bursts of running, and as a result their muscle fibres are short and pale in comparison to those in the dark-coloured muscles of the long-distance-running hare. While the 'bunny hop' is most commonly associated with rabbits, they do have other means of locomotion. Marsh rabbits (*S. palustris*) walk through their muddy habitat on all four feet. Nuttall's cottontail (*S. nuttalli*) will climb 3 metres up a juniper tree to sip dew from its needles, while the riparian brush rabbit (*S. bachmani riparius*), now critically endangered in its home territory in California, will climb to avoid flooding in

Running rabbit.

its river valley habitat. All rabbits swim, though some do so better than others. Marsh rabbits have been found swimming strongly more than 200 metres from shore in the Savannah River in Georgia, USA.[7] The swamp rabbit (*S. aquaticus*), known colloquially in Georgia as the 'cane-cutter', is also an accomplished swimmer, as biologist Charles Lowe recorded:

> On five occasions two men paddling a boat on the study area were unable to overtake a swimming cane-cutter. One individual, when closely pursued by dogs, was seen to dive into the water from a bank several feet high; keeping only its head partially above the surface it drifted with the current to the opposite shore several hundred feet downstream. Swamp rabbits can often outsmart even the best dogs by going from islet to islet and then remaining almost submerged in the water near a log or brush until the danger is past.[8]

In the Eastern cottontail (*S. floridanus*) and the swamp rabbit, the powerful hind legs can propel the rabbit not only forwards but straight up. It is a peculiarity of these rabbits that they engage in a 'face-off' during mating rituals that might involve as many as 30 jumps by the male, as well as squirtings of urine (enurination) on to the doe. Ronald Lockley, a British ethologist, also noted that European rabbits appear to jump for the joy of leaping, as evidenced by one old buck rabbit he observed, who upon seeing a buzzard fly away from his territory, 'suddenly frisked, gave a little jump into the air, twisting sideways so as to come down facing half backwards'. This movement, evidently an important component of a rabbit's escape strategy in flight, struck Lockley as a sign of something else as well: 'The old buck seemed happy. He gave another little jump into the air.'[9]

It is not only the rabbit's body shape that is so distinctive; its long-eared, bewhiskered head is also instantly recognizable. Thin, heavily veined rabbit ears serve to regulate temperature and also swivel to collect sounds. Rabbit eyes are large and protruding and set high in the head, so that they have an almost 360-degree field of vision, with only a small blind spot directly in front of the nose. The nose itself is small, always wriggling as the rabbit sniffs the air using its 100 million olfactory receptor cells (in comparison, the human species boasts only 12 million). In addition, rabbits sniff the air to direct scents towards openings in the roof of the mouth, the vomeronasal or Jacobsen's organ (missing in most human beings). The rabbit has a 'hare lip' that separates, allowing vegetation to be cropped close to the ground. The upper lip sports long vibrissae or whiskers for navigation in the dark, in compensation for the restricted field of vision below the nose. In the rabbit the ears, eyes, nose and whiskers, features common among mammals, are arranged in such a way as to evoke a peculiar affection in its most dangerous predator. As Lockley noted, we cannot help but be charmed by the rounded baby face, the liquid eyes, the delicate ears and the quivering nose. We forget that the rabbit is built not for charm, but for escape.

PRINCE WITH A THOUSAND ENEMIES

'All the world will be your enemy, Prince with a Thousand Enemies, and whenever they catch you, they will kill you. But first they must catch you . . .'.[10] Richard Adams, author of the novel *Watership Down*, did not exaggerate when he called the rabbit the creature with a thousand enemies. In the wild, the rabbit cowers at the bottom of many food chains, pursued by weasels, stoats and ferrets, dogs and cats, snakes and birds of prey. The world's wild cats, from the Iberian lynx to North American bobcats and African caracals, are rabbit specialists. Domestic and feral cats also hunt rabbits as preferred prey, and data from Britain suggests that they kill about ten million rabbits per year. The canids like foxes and coyotes also hunt rabbits, as do all the weasel tribe. Two American biologists assert that 'Cottontails are the meat upon which most North American mammalian carnivore populations are built'.[11] The endangered Amami rabbit of Japan is hunted by feral cats as well as by the mongoose introduced to its island habitat to dispatch the rabbit's only natural predator, a 1.5-metre-long snake. Snakes eat marsh rabbits and cottontails, and in the southeastern United States, American alligators slip unseen up to swimming or resting rabbits. Birds of prey, in particular golden eagles, take rabbits; Audubon pictures a Swainson's hawk (which he calls a buzzard), swooping on a rabbit in one of the engravings in *Birds of America* (plate 372). Even crows prey upon nesting cottontails. Rabbits respond to this heavy burden of predation with two strategies, flight, and a lagomorph *revanche des berceaux*

Fox and Two Rabbits, 19th century, Japanese watercolour.

Eagle with rabbit prey, Issyk Kul, Kyrgyzstan.

Red fox with its kill, a European rabbit.

('the revenge of the cradles', as the extremely high birth rate of French Canadians in response to English Canadian dominance was described in the 1960s).

The rabbit's ability to run, jump and change direction in mid-air enables it to fool its pursuers. In 1939, A. F. Carr kept a pair of hounds at the University of Florida Biology Station at Lake Newnan. For 60 days during autumn and winter, Carr let his dogs loose and was able to observe some 200 rabbit races. Of all the rabbits the dogs jumped, they caught only one, sickly rabbit. Carr described how the marsh rabbit eluded the predators:

> Despite its short legs and awkward gait, the marsh rabbit is very efficient in eluding a pursuer . . . Those which I have watched . . . have all seemed surprisingly unhurried and self-possessed, showing no sign of panic, even with the dogs in full cry a hundred yards behind. The pace is a short hop with numerous short pauses and changes of direction. Two rabbits which I watched back-tracked for some yards and then jumped to the side to continue in the original direction. The hounds continually over-run the trail thus laid, and have to resort to foot-scent in working out its intricacies.
>
> Often an individual will stop abruptly in front of the dogs, hop under a small bush or into a clump of grass, and 'freeze', either in a form or on the bare ground. Strangely, although the scent must lead directly to the spot of concealment, the dogs are usually checked at the place for some time. In one instance I saw them work frantically for fully fifteen minutes before finally routing a rabbit which was all the while in plain view under a palmetto leaf. If pressed closely for a long time, and routed from one temporary refuge after another, the rabbits usually end

John James Audubon, 'Common Buzzard, or Swainson's Hawk', from *The Birds of America* (1827–39).

the chase by taking cover in a hollow log, a hollow tree, the burrow of a gopher-tortoise . . . I found one twelve feet from the ground in the hollow of an ironwood.[12]

Freezing in place, as a marsh rabbit does, is often the preferred choice for rabbits, whose 'agouti'-coloured fur can make them invisible when hunkered down in the dry leaves, grasses and undergrowth of their usual habitats. The 'agouti' hue is the result of changes in colour along individual hairs, from black at the base to yellowish in the middle, then black again at the tip. Since rabbits have three types of hair, and the colour combinations can vary along each hair, the fur itself appears pale greyish, reddish or even dark brown, depending on the habitat. The red rock rabbits of Africa match the colour of their rocky surroundings, while the Mexican volcano rabbit's darkish fur blends with the basaltic rocks of its home among the extinct volcanoes of the Chichinautzin range south of Mexico City. Striping allows the elusive jungle rabbits of Sumatra and Vietnam to move inconspicuously in their shadowy forests. While most rabbits are dark on top, they are paler beneath, an adaptation called countershading that helps to camouflage animals by reducing shadowing that can outline the body. When a cottontail runs, its tail flashes bright white with each bound, which seems counter to its subtle body colouring, but with its zigzagging flight the flashing serves to confuse predators.

With so many enemies, most rabbits lead short and perilous lives. It has been estimated that up to 90 per cent of wild European rabbits die within their first year of life. For an Eastern cottontail, which might live for up to ten years if very lucky, the average life span is fifteen months. Rabbits compensate with large litters and early maturity. The Eastern cottontail can bear litters of up to twelve kits, and since it breeds either while pregnant or shortly

Sylvilagus palustris,
the marsh rabbit,
showing the
'agouti' hue
in the fur.

after delivering, a single doe may have up to seven litters per year. Young female cottontails are fertile at two to three months old. A pregnancy lasts 28 days, and the young are free-living within two weeks.

The Eastern cottontail is a prolific breeder, but productivity among the cottontails is highly variable, and some species, like the New England cottontail, now being replaced in its home range by its southern cousin, have only two or three small litters a year, with an average of just over five kits per litter. Volcano rabbits have even smaller litters of only two or three young, but breed all year round. That North America is not overrun with the more prolific of the cottontails is a tribute to the efficiency of the predator tribe, including rabbit hunters, who take some 25 million rabbits annually (though this total may also include hares).[13]

Not all rabbits are so fecund. The South American tapeti has only one litter per year. Riverine rabbits in Africa produce only one to two young in a litter, just once per year; the Amami rabbit has two litters per year of one or two kits. Both the latter species are endangered, and the Riverine rabbit is considered to be one of the most critically endangered species in the world, with only 250 breeding pairs remaining in the wild.[14]

HABITS OF RABBITS

The ubiquity of the European rabbit has provided most people with their image of the wild rabbit. It is a brown, furry, large-footed, long-eared animal that lives colonially with its family and friends, nibbling grass and raising its large broods in cosy burrows. This image has been reinforced through the popularity of books like Adams's *Watership Down* (1972, made into an animated film in 1978) and films such as *Rabbit à la Berlin* (2009).[15] *Watership Down*, the story of a group of persecuted but free-living rabbits establishing a new colony, was based on the ethological studies described in *The Private Life of the Rabbit* (1964) by Ronald Lockley. His first-hand observations provided a richly detailed picture of the almost human-like social structure of European rabbit communities. Communal living among rabbits is, however, the exception rather than the norm. Most rabbits, like hares, lead relatively solitary lives, coming together only to mate and sometimes to feed.

In the wild, rabbits occupy overlapping territories; in the case of Audubon's cottontail, which inhabits arid regions of the American southwest, the home territory is more than 3 hectares. Male swamp rabbits occupy a similar-sized territory, but the water-loving marsh rabbits live relatively restricted lives, their home ground often limited by waterways to a hammock in a

swamp, or a small, elevated area of less than a third of a hectare. Mature brush rabbits can tolerate one another at a distance of about 7 metres, but any closer can be too close for comfort and results in a chase. Volcano rabbits, the smallest and most primitive of the lagomorphs, hunker down in groups of two to five animals, and the rock rabbits of Africa also live in small groups. Encounters between solitary rabbits roaming through a group's territory may result in either aggression or indifference, unless male and female meet to breed.

Like their lives, rabbits' courtship and mating are brief and intense. A male and female meet, they may sniff at one another, the doe rebuffs the buck, then invites him to chase her, to squirt highly scented urine, or dazzle her with acrobatic leaps, before she finally stops, relents and makes herself available to her paramour. These displays may last for between five and twenty

Young rabbits by a burrow; *Oryctolagus cuniculus,* the European rabbit.

minutes. At their end, the male eagerly grasps the doe with his front paws, and occasionally with his teeth, mounts her, thrusts several times, squeals, then falls over sideways, seemingly satiated with pleasure: 'The male . . . shakes like a jackhammer for about half a minute, gives a screech upon having an orgasm, and usually falls off to one side.' The buck does not in fact swoon; rather, the force of his passion lifts his hind feet off the ground and once the act is done, he falls over since he cannot keep his balance.[16] The active courtship display allows the reluctant female the opportunity to assess her potential partner's fitness as a sire for her offspring. Not only does she observe his agility and strength, but his scent marking and urination perfume the air, conveying chemical clues about his condition and readiness. In some species, such as the European rabbit, as well as the swamp and marsh rabbits of North America, bucks fight to establish a breeding hierarchy, the most dominant males having the greatest access to willing does. Unlike human females or other mammals, rabbits have a biological requirement for energetic foreplay. The chasing, paw-raking, leaping and spraying followed by copulation stimulate the doe to ovulate, which occurs in European rabbits between eight to twelve hours after the act itself.

Once the buck has fallen away the doe once again rebuffs him, but during the breeding season both will mate with other rabbits, and there is evidence that litters can contain offspring from more than one buck. Female promiscuity is less common than similar behaviour in males, but for female rabbits mating with multiple partners may ensure the greatest genetic compatibility and breeding success, with fewer false pregnancies or failed litters. Some rabbits breed year round, but for others there is a definite season. In the northern hemisphere rabbits are of course a sign of spring, and the return of warmer weather, longer days and new growth are essential to rabbit reproduction. The longer

Cottontail courtship: the over-leap.

day length stimulates testosterone production in the bucks, and they become amorous, their testicles re-emerging from inside their bodies. Females become receptive, timing their breeding to the appearance of green grass, tender shoots and, in some cases, young vegetables in the farmer's garden.

Three to six weeks after copulation, depending on the species, the doe retreats to her nest. Not all rabbits nest in the rambling burrows of popular imagination; for many, home is literally under the bramble bush (and in this proclivity for the thorny thicket lies a famous rabbit tale, to be told in another chapter). Rabbits also take advantage of holes dug by others, hollow logs, woodpiles, or natural cavities under stones or roots. Most does dig a shallow birthing chamber, which they line with twigs and grasses and fur torn from their own bellies; swamp and marsh rabbits make their nests directly on the ground, since given their marshy waterside habitats, flooding is a danger.

Birthing is brief, perhaps lasting fifteen minutes. Newborn rabbits are blind, near-naked creatures. Their mother will lick them clean, nurse them and leave. If they are in a burrow she will stop the entrance with dirt, sealing in the babies until her return, or she will simply cover them with grass, leaves and twigs. She returns usually once a day to nurse for three or four minutes at a time; fortunately for the young, rabbit milk is rich, with about four times the fat and protein of cow's milk.[17] Babies fill up quickly, then go back in the dark for another 24 hours. The Amami rabbit has only one kit at a time and nurses once every 48 hours, but unusually, her only offspring accompanies her after leaving the nest. More commonly, at the end of a month or so, the mother, now often pregnant with her next litter, abandons her babies to their own devices. By then they are miniature bunnies, fully furred, with eyes wide open, ready to run or freeze, and to take their chances in the wide and dangerous world.

SPEAKING RABBIT

'Raggylug' by Ernest Thompson Seton is the story of a cottontail rabbit observed throughout its young life in Oliphant's Swamp (now the Rattray Marsh) near Toronto, Ontario. Though born in Britain, Seton lived in North America for most of his life and became one of its pre-eminent writers on animal life. 'Raggylug' was published as part of *Wild Animals I Have Known* in 1898, and the collection was immediately popular, one of a new genre of wild-animal fiction that began to appear at the beginning of the twentieth century. In his 'Note to the Reader', Seton writes 'These stories are true . . . the animals in this book were all real characters'. He acknowledged that he had ascribed to them 'the adventures of more than one of their kind', and he chose to give them voices, for 'Truly rabbits have no speech as we understand it.' He wrote that 'though in telling this story I freely translate from rabbit into English, *I repeat nothing that they did not say*' (author's italics).[18] Seton's fictional accounts landed him in the midst of a celebrated American literary controversy known as the 'nature fakers', to which not only the naturalist John Burroughs but Theodore Roosevelt, big-game hunter and future American president, contributed. Seton's attribution of individuality and personality to a wild animal was hotly contested, and though he went on to win the Burroughs Medal in 1929 for his more scientific *Lives of Game Animals* (1928), his natural-history fictions remained under something of a cloud. 'Raggylug', however, provides a believable account of both the perils facing a young cottontail, and its behaviours in the wild, from freezing, to running for cover, to laying false trails.

Seton said that translating from rabbit means understanding the 'system of sounds, signs, scents, whisker-touches, movements, and example that answers the purpose of speech'.[19] Rabbits do vocalize, but for most species this consists of squeals in extremis or during sex, or grunting either in warning or occasionally in pleasure. Perhaps because rabbits are such silent creatures, the scream of a rabbit in distress is startling. Audubon wrote of the Eastern cottontail, that 'its voice is never heard except when wounded or at the moment of its capture, when it utters a shrill, plaintive cry, like that of a young child in pain'.[20] Swamp rabbits are highly social and more vocal; they have a repertoire of five distinctive calls, from squeaking to chirping to a two-syllable warning call. Rabbits also 'thump' with their hind feet in warning, often for several minutes.

If their speech is limited, their sense of smell is highly developed, and rabbits are particularly equipped not only with highly sensitive noses, but with a number of organs specifically focused on laying down scent markings. Whether free in the wild or kept in the house, rabbits 'chin' objects in their territory. 'Chinning' makes a place smell familiar, 'like home', and both male and female rabbits scent mark with their neck glands. Eastern cottontails and European rabbits also rub a corner of the eye along prominent objects, releasing secretions from the Harderian gland. Inguinal glands, which lie alongside the penis or vulva, are also used in scent marking, as are the anal glands.

Rabbits are tidy animals, particularly when it comes to defecation. They tend to use 'latrines', and the hard pellets that accumulate in these spots are coated with secretions from the anal glands. Female European rabbits often rest on the tops of latrines during the breeding season, perhaps to transfer to their own bodies the scents of the dominant male. Rabbits examine the urine of others as carefully as a urologist, sniffing and squirting at entrances to burrows, at objects in the territory and at each other. The chemical cocktail in rabbit urine identifies gender, age, identity, dominance and condition, one whiff replacing a thousand words of human conversation. The richness of their olfactory world is incomprehensible to the human nose, and even a house well chinned by a dominant house rabbit remains odourless to the homeowner.

Beyond communications with its own kind, the rabbit leaves evident marks of its presence in the wild. The distinctive two-and-two track is often accompanied by equally distinctive piles of dry pellets. Rabbits produce two kinds of pellet, soft and hard.

The soft pellets are created through a fermentation process in the caecum or hind gut, an organ which in humans is called the appendix. The rabbit that appears to be eating its own soft faeces is actually digesting its food a second time. Rabbits consume large amounts of fibrous plant materials, but hind-gut fermentation is not as efficient as a similar process in other mammals like sheep, deer and camels, so rabbits ensure that they receive maximum benefit from their food by eating these soft pellets, full of vitamins and minerals.

Dry pellets reveal evidence of the rabbit's diet in the wild, as do the clipped branches and stripped bark of trees and shrubs. Rabbits are vegetarians and often prefer tender grasses and clovers, but will eat tougher foods if others are not available. A walk in the northern woods will show where rabbits have dined on wild roses and blackberries, raspberry canes, apple, elder and willow. The marsh rabbit nibbles on briars, tupelos and sarsaparilla, while the North American pygmy rabbit has an almost steady diet of sagebrush, which proves toxic to many animals. The forest rabbits eat a wide variety of plants and fruits, and yes, when they can, rabbits raid gardens for cabbage and carrots, turnips and parsley, the stuff of Mr McGregor's garden, made famous by Beatrix Potter, and a preferred food source for the European rabbit.

2 The Natural and Unnatural History of the European Rabbit

'Ruthless invader', 'lethal threat', 'food-chain genocide', 'public enemy number one', 'plague', 'swarm', the 'chainsaw of the outback' – these refer, of course, to the European rabbit (*Oryctolagus cuniculus*), or the bunny. This extravagant language seems disproportionate to the menace posed by a small vegetarian mammal, beloved of children and bringer of Easter treats. How did the European rabbit become classified as an 'extreme pest risk',[1] the enemy in a grim war to prevent the 'eco-annihilation' of Australia, a country 10,000 miles away?

ORYCTOLAGUS CUNICULUS AND HOMO SAPIENS

The story of the European rabbit and its long, complex and interdependent relationship with that most successful of invasive species, the human, reveals much of the ways in which people interact with their animal cohabitants. The principal ancestral home of the European rabbit is the Iberian Peninsula, where the oldest fossils are found, dating to the Middle Pleistocene epoch about 500,000 years ago. In the Roman period rabbits were so commonly associated with Iberia that they became the symbol of the country of Hispania. Coins produced under the Emperor Hadrian featured on the reverse the figure of Hispania reclining, a bunny at her feet.[2]

Despite rabbits' reputation for uncontrollable reproduction, until the Middle Ages the rabbit population in Spain remained relatively restricted to its original territories along the coasts. As biologist John Flux has pointed out, rabbits, 'compared with other camp followers of man such as sparrows, starlings, rats, cats, and mice . . . have been less successful penetrating continents'.[3] While rabbits can and do adapt to differing environments, their continental spread was hampered by ecological constraints: suitable food, habitat and the presence or absence of their many enemies.

The European rabbit is a keystone prey species in the Mediterranean environment, so much so that it is sometimes referred to as a 'rabbit ecosystem'. In this ecosystem the rabbit provides food for more than 40 other species, from snakes to eagles. Despite its legendary fecundity, it is now at near threatened status on its native ground. According to the International Union for the Conservation of Nature (IUCN), 'O. cuniculus populations within the natural range have declined an estimated 95% since 1950, and 80% in Spain since 1975.'[4] Not even the annual release of half a million rabbits by hunter groups in France and Spain has arrested this decline. With this dramatic decrease in the rabbit

Gold sestertius of Hadrian showing personification of Spain with rabbit, AD 134–8.

population has followed a decrease in predators, and in particular the specialist rabbit hunters, the Iberian lynx and Iberian Imperial eagle, now also critically endangered. How can this be? The human species has played a central role in both the natural and unnatural history of the European rabbit.

There is evidence from excavations in Nice that, as early as 120,000 years ago, rabbits were being slaughtered for human consumption. Early human inhabitants of the Mediterranean littoral evidently found rabbits good to hunt and good to eat, and these characteristics accounted for their range expansion from their original sunny corner of Europe to the islands of the Mediterranean. As one biologist points out, 'In comparison with other species, the rabbit is not so much a successful colonizer as a convenient animal to transport'.[5] Neolithic settlers probably brought rabbits to Minorca between 1400 and 1300 BC,[6] and the Phoenicians were later responsible for their shipment around the Mediterranean. During the classical period the rabbit remained a novelty, found only in Spain or on certain islands. Since the hare was common in the Mediterranean, early travellers described rabbits as smaller versions of hares. The Greek

Rabbit and figs, fresco from Herculaneum, c. AD 79.

historian Polybius, however, distinguished the rabbits he saw on Corsica from hares in both habits and culinary characteristics:

> The rabbit indeed at a distance looks like a small hare; but when taken in the hand, it is found to be widely different both in appearance and in the taste of its flesh; and it also lives generally underground.[7]

Their size and their habit of digging underground burrows became defining characteristics. Strabo, a Greek geographer, also described how rabbits were hunted in Spain, using a particular technique involving

> wild cats from Africa, trained for the purpose. Having muzzled these, they turn them into the holes, when they either drag out the animals they find there with their claws, or compel them to fly to the surface of the earth, where they are taken by people standing by for that purpose.[8]

These 'wild cats' were ferrets, descendants of wild polecats (*Mustela*), and their history and distribution is so entangled with that of their prey and their keepers, the human hunters, that one author asserts that their story cannot be told separately from that of rabbits.[9]

While rabbits might be accounted as tasty meals, their food habits and behaviours made their presence a mixed blessing, particularly on islands. Strabo remarked in his *Geography* that on the Mediterranean coast of Spain there were scarcely any destructive animals, 'with the exception of certain little hares which burrow in the ground, and are called by some leberides. These creatures destroy both seeds and trees by gnawing their roots.' He recounted what would turn out to be a cautionary tale about these destructive little hares:

> It is said that formerly the inhabitants of the Gymnesian islands (Majorca and Minorca) sent a deputation to the Romans soliciting that a new land might be given them, as they were quite driven out of their country by these animals, being no longer able to stand against their vast multitudes. It is possible that people should be obliged to have recourse to such an expedient for help in waging war in so great an extremity, which however but seldom happens, and is a plague produced by some pestilential state of the atmosphere, which at other times has produced serpents and rats in like abundance.[10]

The 'vast multitudes' of rabbits produced in habitats with ample food and few natural predators provoked overt hostility in their human neighbours, and the rabbit wars began. In his *Natural History*, Pliny described how Roman settlers had literally called in the army to rid them of the pernicious beast. He noted as well that he had heard of a town in Spain that had been undermined by the *cunicula*, a name given to rabbits because of their propensity to dig tunnels.[11] In these earliest descriptions of European rabbits emerge the themes that continue to dominate our discourse about them today. They are tasty, they multiply and they are a plague, particularly on islands, as we shall see as we follow their spread from the Mediterranean into Europe and the wider world.

'HARMLESS AND GOOD FOR FOOD'

Anthropic dispersal is the term used to describe the role of human beings in the spread of animal and plant species, either by accident or design. The dispersal of the rabbit was most emphatically by design. Rabbits were a ready source of meat at a period when transporting fresh food was a challenge. They were relatively easy to keep, destructive but not savage, and they multiplied. Pliny said that 'It is a kind provision of Nature, in making animals which are both harmless and good for food, thus prolific'.[12] The European rabbit is not only prolific but almost unrivalled in its capacity to convert any kind of greenery into large quantities of meat in a comparatively short time.

The Romans were quick to take advantage of the fecundity of rabbits. It was a simple matter to place Spanish rabbits in their *leporaria*, stone-walled enclosures usually of an acre or two but sometimes of vast extent, which housed hares and often sheep and deer. Within a few months the owners could dine on *isicia de cuniculus*, or rabbit rissoles, or on the even more delicate *laurices*, 'young ones, either when cut from out of the body of the mother, or taken from the breast, without having the entrails removed'.[13]

A few centuries later a quirk of early-medieval canonical interpretation classified *laurices* as 'aquatic', and not being 'meat' they were suitable for consumption on fast days. In the sixth century, Gregory of Tours in his *Historia Francorum* noted disapprovingly the French monks' too evident enjoyment of the delicious *laurices*, but by the tenth century the monks were raising enough rabbits to ensure a ready supply of these tasty treats. They were, however, not the only ones to enjoy a meal of rabbit, and between the tenth and twelfth centuries the French nobility established numerous warrens as both reservoirs of meat and hunting preserves.

The Normans brought their taste for hunting and eating rabbits to Britain in the twelfth century, first installing colonies on offshore islands. By the thirteenth century warrens were established on the mainland in both England and Scotland.

Warrening became a popular form of land use in Britain, where in many areas the soils were too poor for farming but suitable for rabbits, which could subsist on sparse fodder and provide rapid return. The historical geographer John Sheail has mapped almost 400 place names in England alone that contain the word 'warren'. (This total does not include names such as 'Coney-garth', or 'Conery', based on the word 'coney', the original word for an adult rabbit; 'rabbit' referred to the young only.)[14]

By 1555 the celebrated Swiss naturalist Conrad Gesner could write: 'There are few countries wherein coneys do not breed, but the most plenty of all is in England.'[15] Indeed, by the end of the sixteenth century England had become a most rabbit-y country. It was estimated that rabbit warrens and deer parks covered one-twentieth of the land, and that there were more rabbit warrens in England than in all of Europe. By the 1690s, Gregory King in his statistical survey estimated there were ten time more rabbits than deer. The whole of the Brecklands of East Anglia, an area of sandy soils more than 1,000 square kilometres in extent, was described in the nineteenth century as being 'a mere rabbit warren, and still goes by the name of the holely land'.[16] Dry land

A hunting animal (centre) enters a warren mound, from the Luttrell Psalter, c. 1325–35.

was particularly suitable for warrens and, despite sparse vegetation, the rabbits of the Breckland were 'as fat as little pigs'. It
was said that 'conies doe love rost-meat', or dry, sunburned
grasses.[17] Warrens were also located on the British seacoast, the
water providing a natural boundary, and there rabbits fed on
sea purslane or maritime grasses; at low tide in the Orkneys, they
could even be seen out on the flats grazing the seaweed-covered
rocks with their sharp and ever-growing teeth.

The rabbits' preference for dry, light soils may have reflected
their Mediterranean origins, and despite their reputation for
prolific breeding, once transplanted to more northerly climates
they required special care, particularly if they were to return a
profit to the warren keeper. First, they had to be installed in their
new homes. Rabbits were often reluctant to take up residence
on unfamiliar grounds, and would refuse to dig their own holes.
Warreners would bore 'cony holes' and shove the rabbits into
them. They would throw up special mounds of earth, so that

rabbit burrows would be protected from flooding on flat grounds. In some warrens wooden hutches or 'clappers' were built for does, though the keepers acknowledged that the 'clapper conies' were of a 'slumbering disposition',[18] and their offspring were early returned to the free-range life of the warren.

Trees were planted in warrens in order to provide shelter as well as food for the rabbits. In 1605 Olivier de Serres, in his magisterial work *Théâtre d'agriculture et mesnage des champs* ('Overview of Agriculture and Land Management'), suggested that warren keepers plant fruit trees like pears, cherries, apples and almonds, or oaks, since acorns made the rabbits plump. Elms gave the rabbits a peculiarly fine taste, while junipers scented the flesh.[19] In colder winters the rabbits often required supplementary feeding, and keepers would distribute hay, corn, branches, or later turnips and rootstocks among their charges.

The rabbits also needed protection from predators, and warreners watched for and trapped foxes, stoats, polecats, weasels and birds of prey. The most dangerous predator was of course the two-footed variety. Where there were rabbits, there were poachers. In the reign of Richard ii, poachers were alleged to have taken 10,000 rabbits from a warren in Somerset. Laws were enacted to protect the warrens, with severe punishments for those caught with a coney in hand or under arm. In Britain, under an Act of 1765, any person apprehended stealing rabbits during the night (and by definition a poacher) could be transported for seven years, whipped, fined or imprisoned.[20] The severity of such laws did not, however, stop gangs of impoverished rural workers or miners and millhands from wreaking havoc on warrens in protest at their poverty and the restrictive legislation. Feudal laws, such as *le droit de garenne* (the right of warren) in France, which confined the taking of animals to the nobility, had always chafed the peasantry. As rabbits became

Jan Wyck, *Rabbit Hunting in an English Warren*, late 17th century.

38

more numerous in the mid-eighteenth century, these laws began to seem increasingly burdensome and unjust, and the right to hunt rabbits freely acquired symbolic value. During the French Revolution and later during the unrest in Britain in the 1840s, there was popular agitation for the repeal of game laws that penalized the poor and hungry by preventing them from enjoying the 'poacher's chicken'.

THE 'WILD' RABBIT

Early warrens resembled game preserves, with no physical boundaries. As they became more common, stone or earthen and sod walls were erected around warrens not only to keep out predators, but to keep the rabbits in. Not surprisingly, given that their name (*cunicula*) means tunneller, the rabbits easily dug their way out. Water was assumed to be an efficient barrier and warrens were sometimes created in gardens on small islands. One appears in the plans for the garden of Vrijburg Palace, designed for Count Johan Maurits van Nassau-Siegen in Brazil in 1639–42. Surrounded by a moat and connected by a small footbridge, it boasted 'a great multitude of rabbits'.[21] Rabbits can of course swim, and narrow moats were ineffective barriers. Wider moats with vertical banks worked well until a severe winter would freeze the water, and even steep banks could not hold back a determined band of rabbits. Warreners also assumed that rabbits were too delicate to survive long in the wild, but the European rabbit is an adaptable beast.

Given dry, loose soil for burrows, suitable vegetation, respite from predators and a chance to breed, rabbits will flourish. Rabbits may have been living wild in England from the late thirteenth century but they did not abound in large numbers until the eighteenth century. They were living free in France from

the early medieval period, and by 1423 there were wild colonies in Germany, but rabbits were slow to spread into the north, arriving in Scotland only in 1792. The eighteenth-century British naturalist Thomas Pennant noted that 'they love a temperate and a warm climate, and are incapable of bearing great cold, so that in Sweden, they are obliged to be kept in houses.'[22] As a result, rabbits were uncommon in Scandinavia and eastern Europe until the later nineteenth century, when they were objects of deliberate introduction.

The wild rabbit population of northern Europe today is very much the result of human intervention. Captive animals brought in cages and saddlebags and warren escapees were the basis for these populations, which are genetically more related to the domestic stock of priories and hunting preserves than to their wild Iberian cousins.

Until the mid-eighteenth century wild European rabbits were considered a rarity and unexpected resource in most places, though locally they could be accounted a pest. What happened in Britain in the late eighteenth and nineteenth centuries changed popular opinion about the timid rabbit. During this period, as new forms of rural sports became popular, including fox-hunting and shoots for pheasants, partridge and hares, landlords devoted considerable efforts to eliminating 'vermin', many of which were also rabbit predators. Whereas previously predation had kept rabbit populations in check, the persecution of pine-martens, polecats and birds of prey allowed rabbits to breed unhampered by many of their thousand enemies. In addition, gamekeepers began to release rabbits as food for the much sought-after foxes, but the foxes could not keep up with the rabbits' natural increase. The game preserves not only provided protection for foxes but sheltered the prey, and with abundant food, fewer natural predators and improved habitats, rabbit populations exploded. As one of the witnesses reported to a Select Committee of the British Parliament on the Game Laws in 1845, 'I have seen them in the evening as if the land was crawling; it appeared to be all in a crawl.'[23]

Rabbits spread throughout the island, and as the population expanded, so did its impact on the countryside and people's livelihoods. In some rabbit-infested game preserves in Hampshire, the ground was so undermined with burrows that it could collapse under the weight of a horse and rider. Intensively used warrens suffered from severe erosion, and the clouds of sand that blew from them over the neighbouring countryside were likened to desert sandstorms. Hungry rabbits invaded farmers' fields and rural gardens, eating almost everything. By 1900, when Beatrix Potter wrote about Peter Rabbit's raid on Mr McGregor's garden, a density of twenty rabbits to an acre was not uncommon. Rabbits even inhabited central London up until the mid-twentieth century.

While farmers and foresters opted for extermination, rabbit hunters and country dwellers, for whom the rabbit was the poor man's pheasant, preached control. By the early 1950s there were between 60 and 100 million rabbits on the island of Britain, or about two rabbits for every person. The British, like the Romans before them, were ready to call in the army; instead, they resorted to germ warfare. In 1952 a disease pathogen more deadly for rabbits than the Black Death had been for humans nearly wiped out the rabbit populations of Europe, including Great Britain, and it continues to affect population levels today. The story of the myxoma virus and its devastating effects begins in the laboratories of Australia, a continent covered by a 'grey blanket' that threatened to destroy its native species.

THE 'GREY BLANKET' OF AUSTRALIA

There is a special relationship between the European rabbit and islands. We have already noted how European rabbits were brought very early to the Balearic Islands and the resulting problems for the inhabitants (call in the Legions!). Since these early introductions, people have transported rabbits to more than 800 'rabbit' islands worldwide. There is a Rabbit Island off New Zealand and in the Falklands, Coney Island in New York, Isla Conejo near El Salvador and Koh Thonsáy (Rabbit Island) off Cambodia. Islands provided convenient natural *leporaria* or warrens, without the need for stone walls or vigilant keepers.

Rabbits were introduced to virtually every island off the coast of Britain from Shetland to the Isle of Wight, including Skokholm, a small island off the coast of Wales, where in 1927 a young naturalist named Ronald Lockley set up house. Lockley studied the island's rabbits and their history. He noted that in 1325 rabbiters took 'carcases and skins' from the islands of

'A Rabbit Battue
at North Corack',
Victoria, from
the *Illustrated
Australian News*
(April 1879).

Schalmey, Skokholm and Middleholm worth more than £13
(£7,500 in today's currency[24]). In his first year, Lockley and a team
of rabbit trappers took almost 2,500 rabbits by trap, gun and
snare. By 1938, when Lockley attempted to exterminate them
with poison gas, there were 10,000 rabbits on Skokholm's 240
burrow-riddled acres.

Rabbits have been present in the Azores, Canaries, Cape
Verde Islands and the Madeira Archipelago since at least the
fifteenth century, released by settlers or by mariners. The Porto
Santo rabbits, later to be studied by Charles Darwin, were released
by J. Gonzales Zarco in 1418 or 1419, and increased so rapidly
that the human settlers abandoned the island. The Portuguese
or Dutch brought European rabbits to Japan as early as the sixteenth century, and the British took them to Robben Island off
South Africa in the 1650s. As they ventured further and further
from familiar waters, European sailors often left a pair or small

group of rabbits on the islands they touched, with the hope that on their next voyage fresh rabbit might await them or any other 'unfortunate voyagers who might be thrown hungry ashore in this locality'.[25] So James Cook brought rabbits to Motuara Island off New Zealand in 1777, and in 1788 five silver-grey rabbits kept as pets by their owners arrived in Port Jackson, now Sidney, Australia.

Australia is a large island. While the first domestic rabbits in Australia remained peaceably at home, in 1859 a certain Mr Thomas Austin imported 24 wild rabbits from Europe, and released thirteen of them on his estate, to provide a bit of gentlemanly sport. By 1865 he estimated he had shot 20,000, yet 10,000 still remained, and they spread rapidly beyond the boundaries of his land. Australia was ideal habitat for the European rabbit, with dry, sandy soils for roomy burrows, few natural predators and abundant forage, and the population exploded. The first anti-rabbit legislation was passed in 1875, and by 1883 the New South Wales Rabbit Nuisance Act made rabbit destruction not only legal, but the duty of every landlord. Even with active anti-rabbit measures including hunting, trapping, gassing, netting and poisoning, by 1928 the grey blanket had spread across more than two-thirds of southern Australia, crossing the continent at an average pace of 54 km per year, the fastest pace of any colonizing mammal (early rates of spread were phenomenal; 125 to 350 km per year in certain areas). In 1935, David G. Stead, the author of *The Rabbit in Australia*, referred to rabbits as 'The dark stain, that is the rabbit, spreading over the face of Australia.'[26]

The introduction and spread of the wild European rabbit in Australia is 'one of the classic and best-known examples of an invading species'[27] and has turned the charming rabbit of Victorian nursery tales into 'the chainsaw of the outback', competing

Grading rabbits for export, New South Wales, 1880.

with native species and turning thousands of acres into arid desert through overgrazing. Rabbits are credited with contributing to the disappearance of one-eighth of the native mammal population (though their human cohabitants have also played their part in this). A *Threat Abatement Plan for Competition and Land Degradation by Feral Rabbits* lists 156 threatened species that can be adversely affected by rabbits.[28]

Why are European rabbits so successful in Australia? Uniquely in the family, *O. cuniculus* exhibits distinctive social and burrowing behaviour, and the underground warren is the key to the species's success. The light, sandy soils of much of Australia are ideal for burrows, which offer protection from the dry, hot climate and predators. Where the soil is unsuitable rabbits manage with scrapes in the open, and along river valleys farming practices have created ideal conditions for rabbits by providing felled timber for shelter, and succulent introduced grasses and root crops. Among rabbit species, *O. cuniculus* is the definition of prolific, and a single pair can produce 30 to 40 young per year. According to one author,

> Computations have been made, based on average-sized litters (and assuming, of course, that all progeny live and reproduce in the stated time period), resulting in a theoretical total in three years of 13,715,000 offspring from a single pair of rabbits.[29]

In Europe this potentially stupendous reproductive rate had been checked by endemic diseases, parasites and traditional predators. In Australia rabbit-specific pathogens were absent and the native predator population had already been decimated by human activity so that rabbits could reproduce with unusual abandon. And reproduce they did. On his travels around Australia, Mark Twain recorded a conversation with a local resident:

> I already knew a good deal about the rabbits in Australasia and their marvelous fecundity, but in my talks with him I found that my estimate of the great hindrance and obstruction inflicted by the rabbit pest upon traffic and travel was far short of the facts. He told me that the first pair of rabbits imported into Australasia bred so wonderfully that within six months rabbits were so thick in the land that people had to dig trenches through them to get from town to town.[30]

While Twain's informant may have been guilty of slight exaggeration, newspaper reports and scientific literature document the almost unbelievable proliferation of the 'pest' and the equally incredible attempts to eradicate or at least control it. Most famous was the network of three rabbit-proof fences.

At first gardeners put up stone walls or closely spaced wooden posts ('bunny boards') to keep rabbits out of gardens, but by the 1870s it became apparent that the rabbit menace demanded more extreme measures. Between 1886 and 1929, the government and landowners in Australia erected more than 48,500 km of wire fencing to stem the furry tide. Proponents praised the effectiveness of the barriers:

> On the outside of the No. 1 fence there was not a blade of grass to be seen; on the inside there was any amount of grass from three to six inches high and any amount of old feed, while on the outside of the fence the old feed had been eaten down close to the ground and not enough to feed even a bandicoot.[31]

However, despite the efforts of the lonely fence riders, who patrolled on bicycle and camelback, and later by car, the rabbit-proof fence proved no barrier to the tide of rabbits that simply flowed around or under it. The problem of upkeep was exacerbated by a shortage of wire during the Second World War and fences were neglected. After the war, and with the defeat of the Axis, returning soldiers were urged to turn their sights on a new 'Public Enemy Number One'. A newsreel from 1948, 'The Menace of the Rabbit', with its images of sandy wastes, dust storms, rabbit tracks leading brazenly under poorly repaired fences and rabbits swarming like locusts over dry fields, was a call to immediate action in the grim battle against a new invader.

No. 1 Rabbit Proof Fence, which runs North–South through the state of Western Australia.

Cartoon from the *Queensland Figaro* of 2 August 1884, responding to the suggestion that a rabbit-proof fence should be built.

Rabbits at a waterhole, 1938.

Echoing the language of wartime propaganda, the breathless narrator warned Australians that there was 'an army of rabbits heading for the fertile east'. Right-thinking people, not those negligent landlords disinterested in the 'plague' that threatened their livelihood, were called on to enlist in the 'Rabbit War'. Repairing fences, setting traps and poison bait to stem the swarm, gassing and rooting out burrows, and snaring and shooting the vermin were acts of patriotism. The rabbit was 'a foe whose battalions are thousands of millions strong despite unceasing slaughter'. Their formidable reproductive powers made them unstoppable, or as the alarmed narrator exclaimed, 'The amazing fecundity of the rodent is traditional!' Rabbits were vermin, plague, swarming, invading, destroying, ravaging: the enemy at the fence.

While fences are no longer considered the front lines of rabbit control in Australia, the language surrounding the 'rabbit problem' remains unchanged, despite decreases in the wild population and new tools of extermination ranging from more effective poisons to biological warfare. The rabbit is defined as a 'pest animal' throughout Australia, and it is illegal to keep rabbits as pets in Queensland, with Au$40,000 fines for transporting them across state lines, and for selling or releasing them into the wild. Animal Control Technologies, an Australian pest-control company, labels the rabbit an 'environmental vandal', a marauder responsible for the 'wanton destruction of habitat'.[32]

In 2009, *Animal Planet*, a popular nature programme produced for Discovery television, broadcast a segment of its *Weird, True and Freaky* series on a new 'outback invasion' with language even more extreme than that used in 1948. These 'killer creatures' or the 'chainsaws of the outback' posed a lethal threat to

Aboriginal man and child digging for rabbits. Not everyone sees the rabbit as a pestilence.

Australia's environment. The 'furry foes' were raging out of control, committing 'eco-annihilation' and 'food chain genocide'. According to scientists interviewed for the programme, Australia was a 'rabbit petri dish', where like bacteria rabbits could breed, breed, breed.[33] Australians are urged to remain ever on guard against the rise of the 'menace', and in 2012 an online environmental journal warned that once again,

> Two consecutive years of heavy rainfall across much of Australia have triggered a population explosion of crop-ravaging rabbits, which have reached plague proportions not seen since 1995.[34]

Australia is not the only nation that demonizes the European rabbit as a destroyer of the ecosystem. According to *Te Ara*, the

Sheep versus rabbit: Keith Waite, 'Sensational Wool Values', cartoon from the *Otago Daily Times* (16 November 1950).

encyclopedia of New Zealand, there have been a number of lagomorphic ecological disasters on the islands. The first was a rabbit plague that began in the early 1870s and petered out about 1895. Another one occurred in the early 1920s. There was a major irruption and increase in numbers in the 1940s, and the most recent began in the late 1980s.[35]

Rabbits first appeared in New Zealand in numbers in the 1870s, and spread so quickly that at an enquiry in 1876, when asked if he could imagine a method of exterminating rabbits, one witness replied, 'I think it would be impossible to exterminate them; it would be as difficult as attempting to exterminate rats.'[36] New Zealand declared its first Rabbit Nuisance Act in 1876 and created the Rabbit Destruction Council in 1947. Authorities developed the MacLean Scale of Rabbit Infestation, so that landowners could estimate the degree of their problem (a similar

School boys hanging rabbit skins out to dry at Petone, New Zealand, 1932.

tool was developed by the Bureau of Rural Sciences in Australia). In New Zealand rabbits not only caused damage to the soils but, more significantly, they competed with sheep for land. During a rabbit 'infestation' in the 1870s and 1880s, farmers were forced into bankruptcy or abandoned their sheep runs. The rabbits simply out-grazed the sheep:

> Ten rabbits eat as much feed as a 55-kilogram ewe. In 1880 the owner of Earnscleugh Station reckoned his run was infested with over 400,000 rabbits. Until then he had carried about 24,000 merino sheep, weighing about 36 kilograms each. The rabbit population on Earnscleugh equated to more than 66,000 sheep.[37]

A PESTILENCE OF FLESH

Menace, plague, infestation: these are apocalyptic terms. Was it the presence of the rabbits in such numbers ('the land was crawling'), their rodent-like fecundity or their competition for the land itself that made it acceptable not only to describe rabbits as killers and enemies but to seek out control measures that verged on the barbaric? Traditional methods such as trapping, shooting and poisoning were ineffective against the hordes, and a newspaper in 1886 described the government's policies for control of the rabbit in South Australia as 'trying to stop the tide with a pitchfork'.[38] Farmers and landowners demanded pestilence to counter the pest.

Overrun with rabbits, the Prime Minister of New South Wales and his Rabbit Minister devised an international competition for a biological solution to the rabbit problem, with a purse of £25,000 (up to Au$4 million in modern currency).[39] Louis Pasteur, the eminent French scientist, suggested 'something so fatal which

could be communicated, as a contagion, and spread throughout the entire Rabbit population'. His nephew Adrien Loir sailed
to Australia carrying the chicken cholera bacteria (*Pasteurella
septica*), but was prevented by the quarantine authorities from
introducing the virus, for fear that 'A continent overrun with
mad Rabbits would not be a very cheerful place.'[40] Loir's adventures with Australian farmers, French actresses and resilient
rabbits are a brilliant chapter in outback history,[41] but the exped -
ition was not a success for Pasteur's biological agent of choice.

Half a century later, on a small island off Britain, scientists
had fewer qualms about mad bunnies. Ronald Lockley's affectionate and intimate recounting of rabbit life in *The Private Life of
the Rabbit* belied his own work researching rabbit control through
trapping, snaring, gassing and deliberate release of disease. In
1936, a Cambridge scientist approached him to test a pathogen of
surprising virulence on the 10,000 rabbits of Skokholm. The

Louis Pasteur in
his laboratory,
1884.

Rabbit with
myxomatosis.

myxoma virus was first identified at the end of the nineteenth
century in South America, when European rabbits in Montevideo
were killed by a 'new' disease. The virus was endemic in South
American rabbits, but became epidemic in their introduced
European cousins, who had no resistance. (Lockley compared the
plight of the European rabbit to that of the 'Eskimo and other
isolated peoples' when first exposed to the influenza virus by the
white man.)

The release of the virus between 1936 and 1938 had no marked
effect on the rabbit population of Skokholm, since an essential
ingredient – a vector (the rabbit flea) – to transmit the disease
was lacking. This was not the case in Australia. The myxoma virus
was introduced into the wild rabbit population in 1950 and
Australian mosquitoes were hailed as 'flying pins', transmitting

the virus from one rabbit to millions. In arid country, where mosquitoes were scarce, farmers put out traps that contained needles covered with the disease; they caught wild rabbits and rubbed the dried viros on their eyelids; they shot arrows containing vials of infected fleas into the mouths of warrens. In three years, myxomatosis, with its 99.8 per cent mortality rate, had seemingly stopped the rabbit menace in its tracks. Not so in New Zealand, which lacked the vectors of either mosquito or rabbit flea, and where the government was later reluctant to introduce the disease.

Myxomatosis is not an attractive disease. Lockley described the affected rabbits, 'with swollen heads, blind and deaf, and wandering helplessly along roads and fields . . . The blind myxomatous rabbit is a pitiable object.'[42] Australian poet John Kinsella describes an encounter with such an animal on the road:

> . . . The rabbit
> turns towards me. Its eyes tumorous,
> swollen. It targets me blindly . . .
> . . .
>
> The rabbit moves slowly
> into the field, reading the braille
> of pasture, its head rising and falling
> with the tide of stubble.[43]

As it turned out 'myxi' was also not a particularly effective agent for long-term control. As the introduction of the European rabbit to Australia is the classic case of an invading species, so the effect of its most important disease is the 'best-known example of a devastating wildlife epizootic'.[44] After the first epidemic rabbits quickly began to develop an innate resistance to the disease, and mortality rates in some areas of Australia fell from 99 to 40 per cent. Increasingly virulent strains were introduced to the population, but the canny rabbit adapted to a modus vivendi with the virus, and populations once again increased in many areas of Australia.

Forty years after the first release of myxi, scientists began to explore a new and even deadlier virus from Asia. Identified in 1984 by Chinese scientists, Rabbit Hemorrhagic Disease (RHD) spread rapidly across Asia, North Africa and Europe, killing millions of farmed rabbits. They literally bled to death from the inside but, according to researchers, painlessly. Australian scientists imported the virus from Europe in 1991 and began field trials on an island off the coast in 1995. The inevitable happened. The virus jumped to the mainland, and in 1996 the government decided that it was pointless to control the spread and declared the virus a legal biological control agent. They also renamed it Rabbit Calicivirus Disease (RCD), a less graphic appellation. Like myxi, RCD spread through fleas and mosquitoes, and like myxi, it got a little help from its human friends. In New Zealand eager farmers collected the internal organs – in particular the liver, heart and lungs – from rabbits that had died from the disease, minced them in kitchen blenders, covered bait with the diluted slurry and spread it over their farms. As for the rabbits, 90 to 95 per cent died on their first contact with RCD; however, with the resilience of their kind, 60 per cent of rabbits in some areas of New Zealand were showing resistance by 2011. The Invasive Animals Cooperative Research Centre, also known as PestSmart Australia, offers an online downloadable brochure, *Making the Most of Rabbit Haemorrhagic Disease*, to ensure that farmers effectively manage virus release to get 'good kills'.[45]

With the decrease in the effectiveness of biological agents, the human population has once again unleashed a complex battery of weaponry against the menace. Poison, always popular with farmers, remains a weapon of choice. Like Snow White's apple, carrots are spiked with Pindone, an anticoagulant, or 1080 (sodium fluoroacetate), a poison, and spread in areas where 'prefeeds' dropped from aircraft have encouraged rabbits to congregate. Farmers used to hand pump lethal gases into burrows, but now PestSmart offers them a 'roadshow' to demonstrate a carbon-monoxide fumigator as well as proper application of freeze-dried Rabbit Calicivirus Disease for carrots.

Warren-ripping is a vital tool in the destruction of the rabbit. The complex underground burrow that allows European rabbits to survive on the open arid lands 'is the weak link in the rabbit's armour'.[46] Digging it out with shovel, bulldozer or backhoe will virtually eliminate the rabbit population in an area.

Despite the unceasing slaughter, rabbits remain a feature of the countryside of Australia and New Zealand. Moreover, there continue to be people in these rabbit-prone countries who love the rabbit, though at Easter children now search for the colourful eggs brought by the Easter Bilby or savour the chocolate bilbies made by a local company working with the non-profit Foundation for a Rabbit-free Australia. The bilby is a native Australian marsupial with rabbit-like features – long ears, large feet and winsome face. Bilbies, not bunnies![47]

POSTSCRIPT

News of the experiments with a killer virus travelled from Australia back to the original home of the European rabbit. In June 1952, the French scientist Paul Felix Armand-Delille, whose lands were particularly rabbit ridden, procured vials of the myxoma virus from colleagues at a bacteriological laboratory, and inoculated two rabbits caught on his grounds at Maillebois. Within six weeks 98 per cent of the wild rabbits on his estate were dead, and within a year so were most of the rabbits of France. In the autumn of 1953 the disease jumped the English Channel, carried by wild birds, but later farmers deliberately transported sick or dying animals to their lands. However, the rabbits of Britain and France rallied, and their numbers rebuilt until RCD began to spread among the burrows and along the hedgerows. Despite its legendary fecundity, the European rabbit now lives on the thin edge of extinction in its native lands.

3 The 'Useful' Rabbit

In 1884, R. J. Lloyd Price, a well-known British sportsman, published a small volume entitled *Rabbits for Profit and Rabbits for Powder*. His title summed up much of the relationship between people and rabbits in both the Old and New Worlds. The rabbit is useful to its human predators. The flesh is tasty, the fur warm, the skin pliable and the feet lucky. Rabbits' speed and agility make them good animals to hunt, and their domestic arrangements make them easy animals to harvest. Hunting and harvesting define the ways in which people have interacted with rabbits in the wild, and shape the strategies we use to optimize their value and utility to us.

HUNTING RABBITS

Rabbits are good to eat, and for humans they have always been animals of the hunt. When big game has been scarce due to over-hunting or climate change, hunters who in better times may have preferred deer or sheep have turned to rabbits. Due to the prodigious reproductive capacity of rabbits, there are usually plenty to go around. During the most recent ice age, the last of the Neanderthals and the early humans living in the Iberian Peninsula, which remained ice-free, appeared to subsist almost entirely on rabbit.

In the native economies of the New World, particularly in the American Southwest, the cottontail has for millennia been a staple food. Cottontails are swift and agile and their cunning is celebrated in many stories. To bring home a bag of such rabbits is no easy task, and Native Americans devised equally cunning stratagems to catch them. Rock paintings on the walls of small caves in the mountains of New Mexico record ancient hunts. The hunters drove the rabbits into nets and killed them with curiously curved sticks. These 'rabbit sticks' could be thrown in the manner of the Australian boomerang, though the rabbit stick was not designed to return to its wielder. Similar hunts are depicted on the fine ceramic bowls painted by the Mimbre people who lived in southwestern New Mexico more than a thousand years ago.[1] Rabbit was the most important meat source for the Hopi people into the modern era, and they acknowledged the importance of the rabbit drive by calling it simply 'the hunt' (*Màkiwa*).[2] In 1895 a traveller described the annual rabbit drive the Pueblo Indians made at the new moon each autumn. The hunters began with a dance to charm the wily rabbits; then, dressed in rabbit skins, their own skin painted with the outline of a rabbit, they chased the rabbits on horseback, killing them with their throwing sticks:

> Over the broad mesas they charge, hurling their boomerangs with almost unerring aim at the fleeing rabbits; now dismounting to bag their game, and off again with the speed of the wind. They know the haunts of the animals, and divide into groups to surround the likely fields, some routing up the rabbits, while others topple them over with the boomerang.[3]

While the cottontails and jackrabbits of the American Southwest raced across the arid plains, European rabbits had a distinct escape strategy when hunted: they went to ground. The propensity of *O. cuniculus* to dig burrows underlay the success of the warren as a locus for both rabbit raising and hunting. In twelfth-century France the game preserves (*garennes*) maintained by the abbeys or noble houses included deer, hare and other game animals, but by the thirteenth century these warrens were almost exclusively dedicated to rabbits. Early warrens consisted of unwalled expanses of wild land, and the European rabbit, being a domestic creature, was the ideal animal for this type of game park. The doe in particular cleaves to her home burrow, and as long as there is sufficient food and some protection from enemies, the rabbits will settle into the territory of the warren and reproduce as rabbits are wont to do. An illustration by the 'Master of the Conies' (Le Maître des Connils) in the fourteenth-century *Livre de chasse* ('Book of the Hunt'), written by the great French huntsman Gaston Phoebus, depicts a colony of rabbits at ease in such a warren, sitting in the entrances to their holes, frolicking, grazing and washing their

Pieter Bruegel the Elder, *The Rabbit Hunt*, 1560, etching.

faces with their paws. Appearances to the contrary, these rabbits of the warren were not considered domesticated animals and they were certainly not tame. The effects of the chase were in fact to select for the wildest and fastest rabbits. The sport was in pursuing them before they could bolt to their holes. While hares were coursed with dogs by hunters on horseback, rabbits were often hunted on foot, with dogs driving or pursuing them. Rabbits were also taken with bow and arrow, and this hunt was deemed an especial pleasure for women who, like latter-day Dianas, shot at the running rabbits.

Despite supplies of supplemental foods and attempts at control, rabbits easily fled the open warrens for other, greener fields. Those animals that established free colonies in open country earned the ire of the peasants for their depredations on gardens and crops, and while the right to hunt rabbits in the warren was restricted to the nobility, free-living rabbits were targets for

Rabbits at ease in the warren, illustration from a 15th-century manuscript of Gaston Phoebus, *Livre de chasse* (1387–8).

Veit Spierincx,
Two Rabbits,
from an album
of watercolours
of 1637.

hunters from town and countryside. Peter Breugel the Elder illustrates a hunter aiming his crossbow at three grazing rabbits, but his success at capturing more than one with this method might be in doubt.

RABBIT KEEPING

The medieval warren existed not only to provide sport for gentlefolk, but to ensure a ready supply of meat for the noble owners. Rabbits were considered rare beasts in medieval Europe, costing twice as much as chicken, and thus especially fit to grace the tables of the rich.[4] In 1270 the Archbishop of Canterbury supplied 200 rabbits from the abbey warren for the King's celebration of the Feast of St Edward at Westminster.[5] To take rabbits in the quantity required for such feasts required specialized hunting methods, more akin to harvest than hunt. The Romans had imported and domesticated ferrets to chase the rabbit from its burrows in the *leporaria*, and from then on ferreting became an essential feature of warren keeping and rabbit hunting. The 'Master of the Conies' also illustrated a rabbit cull in Phoebus'

Livre de chasse. The warreners stop most of the entrances, then introduce the ferrets into the burrows. Weasels and stoats are accounted the most dire of the rabbit's many enemies, and upon the mere scent of the ferret the rabbits bolt out of the few holes left unstopped, straight into the nets of the warreners.

Roast rabbits appeared on the best tables, heads on, sauced with ginger and verjuice. They were cut up into stews with hare and veal, made into a kind of aspic, or mixed with fried spring onions and breadcrumbs into a 'civet', spiced with ginger, cloves, long pepper, black pepper, nutmeg and cinnamon.[6] Renaissance physicians warned, however, that eating rabbit induced fear and would make a person timid (like a rabbit).[7] This interdiction did not, however, appear to dampen the appetites of the British on their rabbit-ridden island. Thomas Muffet (of 'Little Miss Muffet' fame) wrote a guide to healthy eating that was published posthumously in 1655. Muffet lauds the English rabbit:

> *Connies*, which with us, above all other Nations is so common a meat . . . Here (thanks be to God) they are plentiful, in such sort that *Alborne* Chase affordeth above a hundred thousand couple a year, to the benefit of good house-keeping, and the poors maintenance.[8]

Keeping Britain, and France for that matter, well stocked with these quantities of tasty rabbits demanded new management practices for warrens. Seventeenth-century agricultural experts like Olivier de Serres and Charles Estienne urged landholders to enclose their warrens to protect the rabbits from foxes, wolves and other beasts of prey, to plant cover and browse, and to manage the population density through culling and restocking. Their recommendations in warren management led to a model of rabbit raising that in some aspects continues to be practised today. It

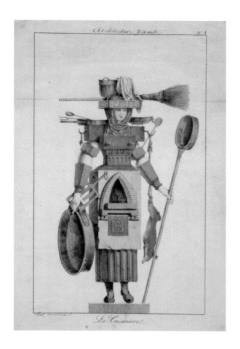

Living Architecture: The Stove, print published by Maison Martinet, Paris, c. 1780–1830.

also led to a means of reproductive control that had consequences for the European rabbit as a species.

What the French experts suggested was that a well-maintained warren had to be stocked regularly with young rabbits to replace those killed by predators or harvested for market. In order to breed rabbits for restocking, farmers could adopt the practice of those early monks, whose taste for *les laurices* led them to devise a particular method of rearing rabbits. To facilitate the easy removal of the newborn, the monks brought female rabbits into the courtyards of the monasteries, confining them to *clapiers*, often simply a walled-off area by the kitchen garden, or a collection of stone-walled or wooden hutches. These *lapins de clapiers* or 'clapper

conies', as the British called them, were serviced by a buck rabbit (usually one male for eight to ten does) and produced litters year-round. Once the young were weaned they were removed to the warren to become wild; if left with their mothers they too would grow docile and heavy, and their flesh would become fatty and unpleasant in taste. However, not all households had sufficient land to support an enclosed warren of several hectares; so, the householder would create a warren in miniature in the courtyard of the house. Here, confined to the yard or sometimes free to hop about in the kitchens, the clapper conies were fed from the produce of the kitchen garden: cabbages, lettuces, escaroles, chicory, chards, fennel, hay and barley all mixed together. (Estienne warned that in some areas they fed the conies on human blood from the blood-letting of invalids, but this, in his opinion, rendered the flesh both insipid and dangerous for human health.[9]) This method of rearing rabbits for the table gave rise in France to a distinction between the warren rabbit and the hutch rabbit, often called a *lapin de choux*, because it was fed cabbage. French gastronomes counselled, however, that too much feeding of cabbage, a plentiful vegetable particularly in winter, would give the flesh an 'off' taste. It was better to ensure that the rabbits had access to hay and oats, chickpeas or sweet herbs, or better still, save them for breeding, and eat only the wild rabbits that roamed the warren or field.

Once established by the mid-seventeenth century, the French method of rabbit rearing became a standard in towns and villages in Europe, including Britain. Rabbits were, as one author put it, the 'town-man's pig', a source of meat and perhaps a sentimental link with the countryside.[10] Breeding all year round and fed on kitchen scraps or grains from small-beer breweries, the virtues of the backyard rabbit were extolled by the journalist and politician William Cobbett in his treatise on rural self-sufficiency,

Victor Gilbert, *The Rabbits' Breakfast*.

Cottage Economy. First published in 1821 in Britain and republished in 1833 in the United States, Cobbett urged rabbits on country labourers:

> Nevertheless, rabbits are really profitable. Three does and a buck will give you a rabbit to eat for *every three days in the year,* which is a much larger quantity of food than any man will get by spending half his time in the pursuit of *wild* animals, to say nothing of the toil, the tearing of clothes, and the danger of pursuing the latter.

Minna Bolingbroke, *The Rabbit Hutch,* 1905, etching.

Everybody knew how to knock up a rabbit hutch and Cobbett could think of nothing green that a rabbit would not eat. Not only were rabbits good to eat, but they were also good for you! This was

particularly true for boys, in whom the care of the economical rabbit bred good habits:

> Of all animals rabbits are those that *boys* are most fond of. They are extremely pretty, nimble in their movements, engaging in their attitudes, and always completely under immediate control. The produce has not long to be waited for. In short, they keep an interest constantly alive in a little chap's mind; and they really *cost nothing*... The *care* is all; and the habit of taking care of things is, of itself, a most valuable possession.[11]

Cobbett's advice was to be often repeated on both sides of the Atlantic, and domestic rabbit kept being touted as a cheap and easy source of fresh meat, as well as a source not only of profit but of pleasure. An American aficionado with the initials H. A. P. wrote to *The Cultivator*, the journal of the New York State Agricultural Society, in 1845, assuring readers that 'a fat rabbit, stuffed and roasted, is not bad to take at any time'. Moreover, the care of his household rabbits had been undertaken

> mostly by children, to whom they afford much pleasure, they grow fat and multiply surprisingly; and their skins supply all the little girls with pretty muffs and various trimmings for their clothes.[12]

Not only were rabbits nourishing and economical, but they gave pleasure to children, and once eaten they could be worn. In the seventeenth century, in his book of tips on how to get rich, Gervase Markham put it succinctly: a rabbit is in essence a 'free lunch', at least as far as the return on its skin is counted. If a householder raised 'rich' conies with blackish fur, the sale of the skins alone would cover the costs of their raising:

they are ever ready at hand for the dish, Winter and Summer, without charge of Nets, Ferrets, or other Engines, and give their bodies gratis, for their skins will ever pay their Masters charge with a most large interest.[13]

The pelt of the rabbit is fragile and soft, and rabbit skins have been associated with babies and children in songs and nursery rhymes like this eighteenth-century lullaby:

Bye, baby Bunting,
Daddy's gone a-hunting,
Gone to get a rabbit skin
To wrap the baby Bunting in.

In 1926, when J. E. Middleton adapted the Huron Carol (*Jesous Ahatonhia*, written in 1643 in the Huron Wendat language by Jean de Brébeuf, a Jesuit missionary and martyr), he may have been thinking of this rhyme, since he describes the Christ child wrapped in 'a ragged robe of rabbitskin'. Rabbit-skin robes were indeed worn by native peoples in North America, most commonly by the rabbit-hunting nations of western North America from the Yucatan up to the Canadian border. These robes were not crafted of pelts stitched together, but rather woven from strips of rabbit skin to make thick, double-sided blankets and capes. It would take a hundred rabbit skins to make a robe, and recent experiments have shown that they were indeed warm, outperforming contemporary sleeping bags and down coats in heat retention.[14]

From the Middle Ages on, European rabbit fur was also appreciated for its warmth and softness. Rabbit skins were exported from their native Iberian home to Britain, France and Belgium,[15] and until the products of local warrens made the fur more widely available, rabbit was considered a luxury fur, forbidden to nuns

and monks, but worn by the nobility and merchants. The fur of
plain grey-brown 'wild' rabbits was used to line women's jackets
and men's cloaks, and among the fashionable there was a demand
for black and silver-grey rabbit fur. Henry VII of Britain appar-
ently went to bed wrapped in black rabbit fur to ward off the castle
chill.[16] As the rabbit population of Britain grew, rabbit pelts became
an important export, and by the fifteenth century British-bred
bunnies had supplanted the Russian squirrel as the basic fur of
northern Europe. British rabbit was also exported to Eastern Europe,
and in faraway China mandarins lined their silk robes with soft
silver-grey furs from the warrens of Lincolnshire.

Not all pelts found their way to the furriers. Some were sent to milliners, where the fur was shaved from the skin and used to make felt for hats, replacing in some measure the more expensive beaver felt. The residue from the felting tanks was used to stuff pillows, being almost as soft as feathers. The shaved skins were sometimes sewn into gloves, or were cut into thin strips ('vermicelli') to be turned into rabbit-skin glue, used by painters for sizing their canvases before the application of gesso or paint. (It was used later in the confectionary trade to make rabbit-skin candies or jujubes.) Rabbit fat (*axungia cuniculi*) was used for liniments, and rabbit brains were rubbed on babies' gums as a sovereign remedy against teething pains (because rabbits have ever-growing teeth?). Finally, fur trimmings and the ears and paws were returned to the land from whence they came, and farmers reported good crops on soils manured with furriers' clippings. So, the rabbit permeated European culture, enjoyed at the table, worn next to the skin or on the head, providing warmth and comfort in bed, and making canvases smooth and tight for their transformation into the masterworks of Renaissance painting, which occasionally included rabbits as its subject.

DOMESTICATION AND THE RABBIT

When the monks of France began to keep their rabbits in the courtyards of monasteries, and the nobles confined their conies in warrens, they unwittingly began experiments in selective breeding. Strange things began to happen to the wild rabbits of Hispania. Where once they were small, they became large, and where once they wore muted coats of grey-brown fur, they now sported black or white fur, or fancy particoloured pelts. In their very bodies, the rabbits began to reveal the effects of their relationship with their human captors and cultivators.

George Edwards,
*A Domestic Rabbit
(Oryctolagus) from
Muscovy*, 1736,
watercolour.

Domestication has profound effects on captive animals. It can result in changes in body size and in the outward appearance of skin or fur colour and texture, in the skeleton, particularly the shape of the skull, and in behaviour. Human keepers deliberately choose certain characteristics or variations, and selectively breed their stock to maintain these variations. Colour variation occurs naturally in European rabbits, and when rabbit populations are concentrated, as they were in warrens or courtyard hutches, it is not surprising to see black rabbits, white or albino rabbits, or silver-grey rabbits, known as *riches* in France.

By the fifteenth century white rabbits were being exchanged as gifts among the nobility, and black-furred rabbits were specifically bred in Britain for the fur trade. Silver-grey rabbits were also highly sought after by furriers for the quality of their pelts. Pied rabbits with black-and-white markings also appeared, and in *Historiae animalium*, the mid-sixteenth-century encyclopedia of all animal kind, the great Swiss encyclopedist Conrad Gesner includes an engraving of a *cuniculo*, which in some editions sports

a multicoloured coat.[17] Warren keepers noted, however, that when rabbits went feral, they reverted to the grey-brown colouration of their wild ancestors, so that those who raised the blacks and *riches* tried to ensure that they bred true by enclosing the warrens or locating them on islands. While some animals decrease in size when domesticated, clapper conies grew large. The celebrated Italian naturalist Ulisse Aldrovandi recorded the appearance of rabbits four times the size of the wild variety at Verona in the sixteenth century.[18]

Clapper conies were, however, as the French noted, of 'slumbering disposition', and a number of authors also remarked that they had lost the 'wildness' of the warren kind. By the early eighteenth century, with the increase of rabbit keeping on farms and in towns, rabbits had become very much domesticated animals. John Mortimer, an eighteenth-century British agricultural writer, suggests that they are best raised in barns, like tiny furry cattle, for the tame Rabbets must lie dry, and warm, or else they will not breed in Winter, which is the chief time of their Profit, and what makes them preferred before the wild ones, and they are much better Meat, if they have their Liberty.[19]

THE 'RABBIT AGE'

While it might be argued that every age is a rabbit age, Mr Lloyd Price, in his treatise on *Rabbits for Profit and Rabbits for Powder*, explained that 'The *raison d'etre* of this little work is that this particular epoch of our existence, the good year 1884, may fairly be entitled the "rabbit age".' Lloyd Price added that 'nowadays, people have got it into their heads that there is money in rabbits, as there certainly is sport'.[20] Flesh, fur, fancy and fun – the rabbit supplied all, and most economically:

Print by Dean Wolstenholme II, *Ferreting Rabbits*, or *The Rabbit Warren*, 1826, after a painting by Dean Wolstenholme I.

Constant Troyon,
Rooster and Rabbit,
mid-19th century.

> The rabbit shares with the fowl and the pig the merit of
> being a save-all – being a transmitter of useless scraps and
> offal into useful and valuable fur and flesh.[21]

During the nineteenth century rabbit meat rose in popularity, particularly in Britain, France and the Low Countries. Once a dish fit for kings, rabbit was now cheaper than beef and the choice of the 'humbler classes'. Rabbits continued to be raised in 'flesh' warrens, but the farmer's rabbit court and pit or the backyard rabbitry of the town dweller were also producing their fair share of rabbits for home consumption. In France and Belgium rabbits were raised for market on a few acres in the village, or in cages in the urban gardens of transplanted countryfolk. The quantities produced were staggering. Not only was there enough to feed the continental appetite for *lapereaux aux petits pois* (rabbit with peas)[22] or the classic 'civet' (*sièvre*), but there was plenty for export

to the rabbit-loving British. The newly urbanized working classes of industrial centres such as Liverpool, Leeds and Birmingham were avid for rabbit, and according to one author, 'a rabbit has only to be exposed for sale in any of the manufacturing towns to be bought directly.'[23] Rabbits were roasted, stewed, baked in pies or curried, and were recommended especially for children. A recipe for rabbit pudding (like a French civet but with ketchup) was featured in a cookbook written for the working classes by the eminent chef Charles Francatelli, the former Chief Cook to Her Gracious Majesty Queen Victoria.[24]

During the mid-1850s, twice-weekly wagons filled with rabbits would be shipped to London from Belgium, amounting to some 26 million carcasses annually.[25] The metropolitan markets were crowded with 'those well-known boxes crammed with a compressed mass of red, shapeless flesh, composed of skinned rabbits', imported from the Continent.[26] Game dealers in Britain could barely keep up with demand for the native product, and in the winter of 1873 half a million rabbits were sold at the markets in Liverpool and Manchester.[27] With the passing of the Ground Game Act in the 1880s, farmers could trap rabbits freely, and they eventually took over the home market from the warren suppliers. Surprisingly, despite the plenty of rabbits in markets and gardens in 1900, shipping tinned rabbit from Australia and New Zealand was a profitable business, and the Antipodeans had of course rabbits to spare.[28]

Though rabbit drives continued throughout the nineteenth century in America, cottontails and jackrabbits were becoming scarcer as farmers demanded control of the populations to reduce their depredations on crops. American agricultural writers urged the European rabbit on their compatriots as a ready source of food and fur, costing practically nothing. Arriving just after the American Revolution, Charles Varlo, a strange and expatriate Englishman, wrote a treatise extolling 'the great profit of RABBIT WARRENS, how to stock them' (accompanied by his recommendations on 'How to put a stop to runaway servants'). He opined that:

There is not ten miles between New York and Virginia, but what here is a proper spot of land for a rabbit warren . . .

And I need not say of what utility it would be to individuals to have such a fund of plenty dispersed over the country, and that raised from the worst land.[29]

Evidently some Americans heard the call. Caleb Bement, who had begun breeding rabbits as a boy, was an enthusiastic rabbit fancier and promoter:

The real value of the rabbit to man is greater than would appear at first sight. Independently of the fur, which enters largely into the manufacture of hats and other articles, the skin makes an excellent glue. If the flesh is not particularly nutritious, it is a light and agreeable article of food; and none but those who have lived in the country, and have received the unexpected visit of friends to dinner, can form an adequate idea of the convenience of having a plump rabbit or two at hand in the hutch.[30]

Breeding rabbits
in hutches,
France, 1928.

'Turn In Your Rabbit Pelts! The Army Needs Them!' Poster from the War Pelts office (Kriegs-fell), Berlin, 1917.

While rabbit did not occupy the same importance in American cuisine, by the 1880s producers in the United States were exporting rabbit flesh and, more significantly, Americans were wearing rabbit.

By the end of the nineteenth century, rabbit fur was big business in Europe. In Belgium and France 'rabbit skin merchants' collected pelts from private breeders.[31] The pelts were either dried and sold as fur, to be worked into garments, or 'carroted', the fur removed from the skin to be used in the millinery and felting industries, the skins then boiled for rabbit glue and jujubes.

War amputees raising rabbits at the New Zealand military hospital at Walton-on-Thames, Surrey, 1918.

The paws and ears were fed to chickens and other animals, or used as fertilizer. Rabbits became key ingredients in coats, hats, toys, piano keys (felt on the hammers), slippers, baby blankets and, of course, lucky rabbits' feet. Rabbit fur does not wear as well as high-end furs, but it was plentiful, inexpensive and warm.

In 1891 a reporter for the *Fur Trade Review* noticed a day labourer walking down 5th Avenue in New York, warm in his fur-lined overcoat, the skins a by-product of the rabbits his family had eaten.[32] By the 1920s the flapper generation was besotted with rabbit fur. It was cheap, cheerful and could be made to look like mink, seal, beaver or ermine. Rabbit-skin coats were marketed as Minkony, Roma, Electric, Red River or Semeuse Seal, Seal Musquash, Ermiline or Ermilinette, French sable, chinchilla, cat or plain old coney. White rabbit pelts (like New Zealand whites) were in particularly high demand since they could be sheared and dyed, but other fur could be used without dyeing, particularly that of the chinchilla rabbit. The American breeder Edward

Sewing furs, rabbit skin industry, France, 1909.

Children oiling rabbit skins, France, 1909.

Stahl claimed that the dusky rabbit ('The Chinchilla Way Makes Rabbits Pay') was 'the most marvelous fur discovery in the history of fur farming'.[33]

The angora rabbit is a very special breed, raised not for its flesh or skin but for its long, silken 'wool' or fur. First described in the eighteenth century as the 'white shock Turky Rabbet',[34] angora gained great popularity in the 1930s as a fashion fibre for women's sweaters and evening wear. A *Life* magazine article in 1938 showed 'bright young things' and 'Hollywood ladies' sporting angora boleros and muffs.[35] Angora wool also came to the attention of Heinrich Himmler, leader of the ss, the Nazi paramilitary group responsible for, among other things, the running of concentration camps during the Second World War. Between 1941 and 1943, the ss carried out a strange experiment at 31 stations all over Germany, including Dachau, Buchenwald and Auschwitz, the infamous death camps for Jews and other 'undesirables'. While the prisoners starved, angora rabbits thrived under the care of dedicated ss teams:

> Thus, in the same compound where 800 human beings would be packed into barracks that were barely adequate for 200, the rabbits lived in luxury in their own elegant hutches. In Buchenwald, where tens of thousands of human beings were starved to death, rabbits enjoyed scientifically prepared meals. The ss men who whipped, tortured, and killed prisoners saw to it that the rabbits enjoyed loving care.[36]

The angora breeding project, a strange twist on other Nazi eugenics experiments, was aimed at providing a source for thermal

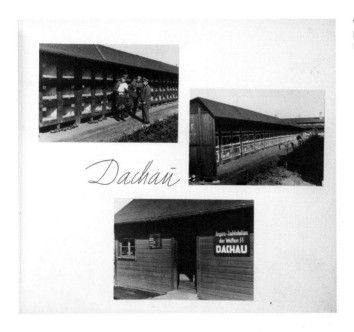

fibres to keep German soldiers warm and dry. By the end of 1943,
25,000 rabbits had provided 4,730 kilograms of wool knitted
into booties, long underwear and briefs. Their service had been
documented in a lavishly illustrated book, bound in woven angora
wool, and dedicated to Reichsführer Himmler by his ss forces.
Before his capture Himmler attempted to hide this book, the evidence of a strange obsession, but it was discovered after the war
by an American reporter. At the end of the war the long rows of
hutches were abandoned, the rabbits likely gone to stew, but
the eerie photographs remain: rows of hutches like barracks (the
rabbit army at the service of the state); the jack-booted officers
holding fluffy white rabbits; sheared bunnies being weighed by
men in lab coats; close-ups of rabbit shears with sinister echoes of

Adolf Hitler and Eva Braun inspect the bunnies at their summer villa in Berchtesgaden in the Bavarian Alps, 1940.

instruments of other tortures; a smiling woman in gay summer clothes posing beside the bags of rabbit wool at Dachau . . .

THE RABBIT BODY

The European rabbit is a mutable beast. Not only is its fur colour and texture variable, but if bred in small groups strange anomalies begin to occur. Some of these are pleasing to the eye, some odd. There are rabbits with short ears, long ears, pendant ears, one ear, no ears, thick coats, woolly coats and silky coats, and giant rabbits weighing five times as much as the lithe warren rabbits. Charles Darwin, who studied variations of animals under domestication, devoted a whole chapter to rabbits, and was especially interested in how parents passed their characteristics along to their progeny. Lops, for example, did not always breed true, and lop-eared parents may produce bunnies with both ears upright, one ear down (the half-lop) or ears sticking straight out the oarlap).[37] This variability and uncertainty turned rabbit breeding from work into sport. By the 1850s rabbits had joined the ranks of the other animals bred to human standards – dogs, horses, cats, mice and pigeons – and exhibited to tickle the 'fancy' of their owners. The lop-eared rabbit was the 'King of the Fancy', and according to Luther Tucker, editor of the *Country Gentleman*,

> Clubs and societies abound for the breeding and exhib-
> ition of the 'Fancy-Lops' . . . Much pains have been taken,
> and much money spent, to bring them to their present
> perfection in form, color and size; all which are minutely
> attended to, and not very easily combined in any one ani-
> mal, and hence they form an admirable test of skill on the
> part of the breeder.

Fancy rabbits in fact allowed the breeder to assume if not a god-like power over mute nature, at least the power of the artist to create novelty:

Thomas Williams, 'Lop-eared Rabbit', illustration from *Every Boy's Book: A Complete Encyclopaedia of Sports and Amusements* (c. 1843–62).

In relation to the man of leisure and science, I would remark that, as the artist delights in the power of moulding the inert clay into life-like form, so does the intelligent and amateur breeder, find infinite pleasure in the yet higher, and more difficult art, of modelling the live material into its most symmetrical proportions . . . To myself the rabbitry is a 'Studio,' whereof the material is cheap, rapidly produced, soon perfected, very abundant, and occupying a small space, and is thus brought under my own immediate care and observation, with but little trouble; requiring months, only, instead of years, to *practically test* theories and speculations, and for studying some of the most important, but not understood, laws of nature.

There is an uncomfortable foreshadowing in Tucker's description of his 'Studio' work to the controlled experiments of the eugenicists, who a half-century later would ask about human breeding many of the same questions Tucker posed about rabbits, such as: 'How far it may be safe to use close affinities? And if deteriorating, what are the first and warning symptoms? In what order does the animal structure give way under a persisted course of such breeding?'[38]

In the Victorian heyday of the fancy, however, people were mostly concerned about the aesthetics of breeding for show. Caleb Bement delightedly described the 'dewlap' on a show rabbit: 'The rabbit looks as if it had put on a fur tippet . . . serving also as a cushion for the chin to rest upon, when "Bunny" is enjoying its afternoon's doze.'[39] Rabbits with particular markings like a 'blue butterfly smut' around the nose, or a 'chain' of dark stripes around the neck, were particularly prized. Size also counted, and in Belgium, breeders produced an enormous meat rabbit known as a 'Belgian Hare'. This was introduced to the United

States in 1888 as a show rabbit, and launched the 'Great Belgian Hare Era'. By the end of the century there were 600 Belgian Hare rabbitries around Los Angeles. Their owners were convinced that they had at last found a bunny profitable to show and to eat. Beatrix Potter, of Peter Rabbit fame, acquired a Belgian Hare in 1889. She called him Benjamin Bouncer and he was her first rabbit model, sitting for a series of Christmas cards. The Belgian Hare craze inspired a generation of rabbit breeders, and by the 1930s there was also the American, the Checkered Giant and the Flemish Giant. In 1928 the United States established its first and only rabbit experimental station in Fontana, California, which lasted for almost 40 years. Converted to a senior citizens' home in 1965, the only evidence of its former inmates is a historic

Mrs J. R. Band and Her Large White Rabbit, 1911.

plaque commemorating the station's contributions to 'new techniques of rabbit care and breeding'.[40]

During the 'Rabbit Age', the rabbit body became not only a palette on which the breeder mixed colours and shapes but also the object of sport. Victorian shooting parties in Britain recorded bags of thousands of rabbits. The record probably belongs to a certain Lord Stamford of Leicestershire, who on a fine day in 1861 went out with 'thirteen guns' and bagged 3,333 rabbits.[41] When the British Parliament passed the Ground Game Act of 1880, giving tenant farmers the right to shoot rabbits on their own land, sportsmen feared that the rabbit population would be decimated as farmers revenged themselves on the crop-ravaging rabbits. Sportsmen of means reacted by establishing special 'game warrens'. Isolated from towns and railways (and from the threat of poachers) the warrens were managed to provide a 'pleasurable excitement' to the hunter. Keepers would go out before the shooting parties, ferreting rabbits from their burrows, then 'sulphuring' the holes by dipping sticks in a noxious-smelling mixture, setting them alight then inserting them into the holes, 'to stink the rabbits out'. The rabbits, whose lives are so much ordered by scent, would not return to their evil-smelling holes, even when confronted by the lines of hunters and dogs. They died in the open, huddled under bushes and clumps of grass; as one enthusiast noted, 'if bunny escapes the first barrel or two, someone else is sure to nail him, as all holes are blocked, and there is no escape'.[42]

Americans also enjoyed their rabbit hunts, and the Eastern cottontail's speed and cunning made it a desirable game animal. Beagles were imported from Britain to run the rabbits much as they did in the game warrens of the old country. Eastern cottontails were even shipped across state lines to ensure suitable hunting stock. The popularity of rabbit hunting at the end of the nineteenth century makes Thomas Austin's unfortunate introduction of those 24 rabbits to Australia more understandable. The Rabbit Age set a pattern for how we think about and behave towards rabbits that has continued to the present day. Rabbit is on our menus and increasingly in our wardrobes. For many people, rabbit is also in our hearts and minds.

4 Rabbit in Mind

Out walking I startled a cottontail. She bolted, all fur and flashing tail, then stopped still and turned her head to look at me, and she saw me, through and through. I could not move until she turned, and with a single great leap, vanished. There is something uncanny in the eye of the rabbit, both recognition and otherness in that penetrating gaze. The rabbit looks you in the eye, and demands that you look back. For a moment, a heartbeat, something akin to recognition and great sorrow flickers and is gone. Does the rabbit remember some deep edenic past when we walked together in gardens? Do we remember conversation? Do we long to speak in the tongues of birds and beasts? Or do we simply wish to be present, in the way that the rabbit is overwhelmingly there, alive, quivering, a token of a world most decidedly not human?

Rabbits occupy a surprisingly large place in the human imagination. Their ubiquity, their almost comic (in human terms) appearance, combined with their strange and troubling presence, have made rabbits members of a select group of animals significant in human culture worldwide. People talk about rabbits, they use them as signs and tokens, they carve them in wood and ivory or bone, or draw their likeness, and they make up stories about them. The rabbit has entered deeply into the human imagination, because of what it is and because of what it might represent.

Everyone knows the rabbit, and its ubiquitous presence makes it a good choice for an animal to symbolize the passing of time and season. Throughout much of Asia, the rabbit or hare is one of the twelve animals of the lunar zodiac, where its season is spring and its hour dawn. The rabbit is also one of the animals in the Aztec calendar, and it is an Easter Bunny that signals the coming of spring for many Europeans. In Asia the Year of the Rabbit[1] arrives every twelve years, and the person born in a Rabbit Year is said to share the characteristics associated with the calendar animal:

> Rabbits are articulate, talented, and ambitious . . . They
> are virtuous, reserved, and have excellent taste. People

Rabbit's eye.

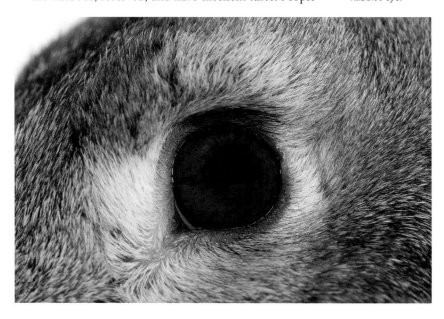

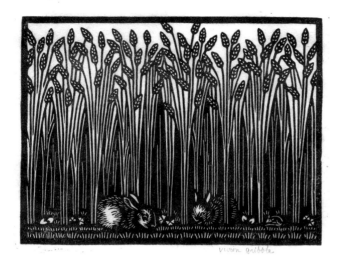

born in the Year of the Rabbit are admired, trusted, and are often financially lucky. They like gossip, but are tactful and generally kind. Rabbit people seldom lose their temper. They are clever at business and, being conscientious, never back out of a contract. They make good gamblers for they have the uncanny gift of choosing the right thing. However, they seldom gamble, as they are conservative and wise.[2]

Rabbit is clever, lucky and gentle, and these traits helped him win a place in the Chinese zodiac. The Jade Emperor declared a contest to determine which animals should rule the calendar. He demanded that the animals cross a swift river to join him. Some animals swam and others flew, but Rabbit hopped from stone to stone, only to land at last on an unstable piece of wood. Suddenly Rabbit felt a warm breeze that pushed his log to the bank.

Dragon, impressed by Rabbit's gentle and considerate nature, had blown him to safety.

The Japanese also tell tales of Rabbit, and they picture him (and occasionally her) in the special cards or *nengajo* sent by post to celebrate the New Year. The postcard tradition began in the Meiji period at the end of the nineteenth century; every twelve years from then on, designers and artists drew running and dancing rabbits, and rabbits reading newspapers or riding bicycles, or depicted scenes from traditional folktales featuring rabbits. Some cards depicted 'snow rabbits', little rice cakes in rabbit shapes, given at New Year's. The word for rice cake is *mochi*, and the word for rabbit *usagi*. It is said that when the farmers of Mount Yahikoyama complained to the God of the Mountain about his rabbits eating their crops, the god intervened and made his rabbits promise to behave (a circumstance that definitely required divine intervention). In gratitude, the farmers offered

Traditional Chinese paper cut for the Year of the Rabbit, 2010.

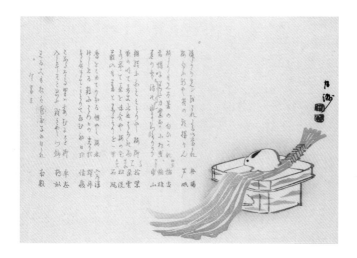

Gesshu, *Usagi Mochi*, New Year's *surimono*-type woodblock print of a traditional Japanese rabbit confection, 19th century.

the deity 'beneficial' rice cakes, or *usachi mochi*. The pun was too delicious to resist, and *usachi* became *usagi*, and rice cakes assumed their rabbity form. The Japanese also associate the rabbit with the moon, as do many peoples, and herein lies another story of rabbits, rice and fire.

THE RABBIT IN THE MOON

Yoshitoshi Tsukioka (aka Yoshitoshi Taiso), *The Monkey King Fighting with the Jade Moon Rabbit*, 19th century, Japanese woodcut. Illustration to the famous Ming Dynasty novel *Journey to the West*.

In many cultures the rabbit has found a place in heaven. Where Europeans saw a man in the moon when they looked at the dark blotches on its imperfect surface, others saw a rabbit or a hare. In China the moon rabbit is the companion to a captive princess, and endlessly pounds herbs to make the elixir of immortality. Li Bai, the celebrated eighth-century Tang poet, laments that the rabbit works for naught, since the brevity of human life, the short passage from dust to dust, has no remedy, on earth or in heaven:

98

The living is a passing traveler;
The dead, a man come home.
One brief journey betwixt heaven and earth,
Then, alas! we are the same old dust of ten thousand ages.
The rabbit in the moon pounds the medicine in vain;
Fu-sang, the tree of immortality, has crumbled to
    kindling wood.[3]

To Chinese alchemists the pale Jade Moon Rabbit embodied the Yin or female principle that was associated with the moon not only in Asia but in the West, where the moon is often referred to as feminine. Although associated with spring in the zodiac, the lunar rabbit also became the animal symbolic of the Moon Festival in the eighth month, and when Chinese families gathered to view the full moon, if they had sufficient means they wore robes embroidered with the white Moon Rabbit.[4] In Japan the rabbit pounded and pounded with his mortar and pestle not the herbs of immortality, but the rice for the *mochi* cakes exchanged at New Year. The rabbit was also a lunar animal in the New World, linked among the Aztecs not only with the moon but also with drunkenness, perhaps another form of elixir. At dawn, however, the rabbit was torn to pieces by the great sun eagle, only to reappear at moonrise.[5]

How did the rabbit arrive in the moon? In Buddhist legends the rabbit acquires a saintly air. The Buddha has been reincarnated as a hare or rabbit and Lord Indra is determined to test his virtue. Disguised as a brahmin, he asks the animals to bring him food. Some bring fish and curds and honey, but the rabbit, who browses the grass, has only himself to offer. He flings himself into the fire to offer his very body as the brahmin's supper. To immortalize this selfless act, Indra makes the figure of the rabbit on the moon. There are many versions of this tale, some in which

the Buddha himself places the virtuous rabbit in the moon. It is not only in India that the rabbit is associated with fire. In Aztec legend the rabbit must also pass through fire before arriving in the moon. Fire in the body becomes fever, and pious Buddhists in Japan purchase paper icons of the ever-pounding rabbit and the bodhisattva *Monju* (the embodiment of law and wisdom

and patron of people born in the Year of the Rabbit) to reduce high temperatures and cool the body.

The Ainu people, who live in the snowy islands of northern Japan, also tell a story of how the hare got his white coat and black feet. The children of the sky were pelting each other with snowballs, which fell to earth through the holes in the clouds. As they fell the God of the Sky batted them with a torch, burning their toes and ears, and now the hares have coats as white as snow, with black-tipped ears and little charred feet.[6] In *Inaba no shirousagi* ('The White Rabbit of Inaba'), a famous Japanese folktale, poor Rabbit is tortured by evil princes whose bad advice burns his skin (and rescued by the youngest prince whose good heart wins him Rabbit's gratitude and the Princess of Inaba).

Rabbit also uses fire for his own ends. In *Kachi-kachi Yama* ('Fire-Crackle Mountain'), Rabbit befriends a farmer whose wife has been murdered and made into stew by a mischievous *tanuki* (Japanese raccoon dog). Rabbit slyly promises Badger parched beans if only he will carry dry straw up the mountain. Tanuki agrees, and Rabbit sets the straw alight. Tanuki 's back is burned, and Rabbit, perhaps avenging his own mistreatment at the hands of the wicked princes, provides Tanuki with an ointment laced with red pepper, an agonizing cure.[7] When Tanuki's back is healed he seeks to best Rabbit in a boat race. Clever Rabbit has made his boat of wood, while Badger's boat is made of clay. Once the clay boat starts to sink, Rabbit kills Tanuki with a blow to the head, and the farmer is at last avenged.

TRICKSTER RABBIT

While the moon rabbit embodies gentleness and self-sacrifice, these are not the qualities usually associated with the rabbit of folk and fairy tale. *Kachi-kachi* Rabbit is more the norm, ingenious and vengeful, tricking his enemies, punishing without remorse. Rabbit is not to be tamed; he is wild and scornful, as he dances beneath the moon.

Song of the Rabbits Outside the Tavern

We who play under the pines,
We who dance in the snow
That shines blue in the light of the moon
Sometimes halt as we go,
Stand with our ears erect,

Our noses testing the air,
To gaze at the golden world
Behind the windows there.

Suns they have in a cave
And stars each on a tall white stem,
And the thought of fox or night owl
Seems never to trouble them,
They laugh and eat and are warm,
Their food seems ready at hand,
While hungry out in the cold
We little rabbits stand.

But they never dance as we dance,
They have not the speed nor the grace.
We scorn both the cat and the dog
Who lie by their fireplace.
We scorn them licking their paws,
Their eyes on an upraised spoon,
We who dance hungry and wild
Under a winter's moon.[8]

The American poet Elizabeth Coatsworth divined something of
Rabbit's true character, his disdain for convention and delight
in his own speed and cunning. It is that spirit that informs many
of the stories told of Rabbit the Trickster, of Cunnie Rabbit, Bugs
Bunny or Brer Rabbit, the rabbit who runs through the jokes
and comic tales of the American South. Rabbit is Dancer and
Messenger, playing his fiddle in the graveyard on a moonlit
night, calling the animals to dance. He is swift of foot and sharp
of mind and full of mischief. When Fox or Wolf or Coyote or
Lion come looking to eat him, he promises a much better meal.

la vitesse des Lapins

He leads them to a pool, or a river or a well, and shows them just
beneath the water a delectable morsel, so round and white, sometimes a wheel of cheese, sometimes a tortilla. If only they drink
all the water up, they will be able to eat their fill. They drink and
drink until their stomachs burst, leaving Rabbit free to admire
the reflection of the full moon shining on the water.[9]

Joel Chandler Harris, who brought Brer Rabbit to print, grew up fatherless in Georgia, listening to the tales told by the black servants on the plantation where he worked as a young man. He listened to those stories with a journalist's ear and in 1881, when he had established himself as a newspaperman, he published a book, *Uncle Remus, His Songs and His Sayings: The Folk-lore of the Old Plantation*. That book was to transform ideas about the cultural heritage of African Americans and was to have a far-reaching influence on a young, rabbit-loving woman in Britain. At the height of his popularity Harris rivalled Mark Twain, and his recounting of the tales of Brer Rabbit, Brer Fox, Brer Bear, the tar baby and the briar patch, made the figure of the devious, boastful, lazy, rogue-hero rabbit a mainstay in American popular culture. Harris was well aware of the rabbit's symbolic weight for his Black American narrator. He wrote:

Kawanabe Kyōsai (attrib.), *Monkey as a Manzai Dancer, with Rabbits Dancing*, 1876.

it needs no scientific investigation to show why he selects as his hero the weakest and most harmless of all animals, and brings him out victorious in contests with the bear, the wolf, and the fox. It is not virtue that triumphs, but helplessness; it is not malice, but mischievousness.[10]

The *Uncle Remus* stories were retold in Disney's animated feature film *Song of the South* (1946), but that retelling was criticized for its emphasis on the humorous side of the stories, rather than their evident social critique. More trenchant criticism of the stories was sparked during the Civil Rights Movement, when African American scholars saw in Harris's appropriation of dialect, and the stereotyped figures of Uncle Remus and the white boy, a celebration of the values of slavery. More recent scholarship has acknowledged Harris's important role in preserving an oral tradition whose roots stretched back two centuries, and has also recognized that Harris himself was aware of what a troubling and contentious message emerged from the tales of ol' Brer Rabbit.

Besides the story of Brer Rabbit and drinking the moon, there are two stories that are widely spread in variants across Central America and the southern United States, both among African Americans and Native Americans. Brer Rabbit is sometimes just too clever for his own good. He is also greedy, and cannot resist the easy pickings in Brer Wolf's garden patch. When night after night Brer Wolf finds his garden raided, he is determined to catch the thief. He makes a figure out of straw and tar. Brer Rabbit arrives for his nightly feast and sees a dark 'gal'. No matter what he says, she stays silent and ignores him; so, Brer Rabbit strikes the tar baby a blow, and his paw sticks tight. Eventually Brer Rabbit is stuck by all four paws and his head, and there is no escape when Brer Wolf comes by next morning. Brer Wolf cannot quite decide how to kill his captive. Should he hang him, roast him, drown him or skin him? Brer Rabbit pleads:

> Oh Maussa Wolf, do don't do me so, but le' me beg you. You ma' roas' me, you ma' toas' me, you ma' cut me up, you ma' eat me, but do, Maussa Wolf, what-ebber you do, don't trow me in de brier bush. Ef you trow me in de brier bush I gwine dead![11]

Master Wolf, seeking to give the rabbit the worse possible death, throws him in the briar bush, from whose thorny depths Brer Rabbit taunts that he and his whole family were 'born in the briar bush', and he once again escapes his just desserts.[12] Brer Rabbit also escapes certain death by persuading Brer Fox to fatten him up and throw him out on the coldest day of the year, a sure way to kill him in the most painful manner (!):

> So Brer Fox he open de pen an' take Brer Rabbit out, an' put him down on de snow, an' den he sot down on de doorstep see him die; but Brer Rabbit he ain't got no notion dyin' jes' den, so he say: 'Oh, you great big fool, dis here jes' what I been use to all de days of my life.' An' he go off through the bushes lickety split.[13]

Brer Rabbit is also of course known for his speed, and the classical fable of the race between the hare and the tortoise is retold in the Americas, both among African American and Native communities. This time, however, it is not the rabbit's indolence and arrogance that proves his undoing, but the way in which Brer Turtle's relations band together to trick the rabbit, with a different turtle (all of the turtles bear a strong family resemblance) stationed at each point in the race.

THE CABBAGE PATCH

Brer Rabbit bears more than a passing resemblance to another
literary bunny who has remained famous since his first appearance in Mr McGregor's garden in 1902. Beatrix Potter not only
kept rabbits as pets, but also read and illustrated the *Uncle Remus*
stories. Harris's subversive rabbit became her reference point
as she created her own world where animals talk, and rabbits
and people intersect.[14] Where Brer Rabbit went 'lippity-clippity,
clippity-lippity' down the road, Peter hops along 'lippity-lippity'.
Unlike Brer Rabbit, however, the tales of Peter and his extended
family were written for children. Peter is naughty rather than
amoral, and disobedient rather than cunning. His father ended
up in a pie, and his cousins the Flopsy Bunnies almost share the
same fate when captured by the irate farmer and shoved in a sack.
A great deal of the charm of the 'bunny books', whose success
amazed Potter and her publishers, lies in the illustrations, in
which Potter placed her rabbits in the gardens and countryside

she herself knew well. She drew from live models, notable among them Benjamin Bouncer and Peter Piper, whom she occasionally drugged with hemp seeds, an intoxicated rabbit being a better sitter.[15] She was an acute observer of the character of her sitters, whose antics and behaviour informed that of her bunny protagonists. She wrote about her first pet in 1892, a decade before her literary success:

> Rabbits are creatures of warm volatile temperament but shallow and absurdly transparent. It is this naturalness, one touch of nature, that I find so delightful in Mr Benjamin Bunny, though I frankly admit his vulgarity. At one moment amiably sentimental to the verge of silliness, at the next, the upsetting of a jug or tea-cup . . . will convert him into a demon . . . He is an abject coward, but believes in bluster, could stare our old dog out of countenance, chase a cat that has turned tail . . . Benjamin once fell into an Aquarium head first and sat in the water which he could not get out of, pretending to eat a piece of string. Nothing like putting a face upon circumstances.[16]

The Tale of Peter Rabbit was a publishing sensation, with more than 56,000 copies of the small-format book in print within a year of publication. Potter often wrote two books a year to meet the demands of her publishers, Frederick Warne & Company, but she soon tired of what she referred to as the 'interminable rabbit stories'. Public demand, however, resulted in the *The Story of Benjamin Bunny* in 1904, *The Story of a Fierce Bad Rabbit* (written for a little girl who demanded a story about a truly naughty bunny) in 1906, *The Tale of the Flopsy Bunnies* in 1909, *Peter Rabbit's Painting Book* in 1911 and *Peter Rabbit's Almanac for 1929* in 1928. The latter two publications are testament to Potter's marketing acumen. She produced a Peter Rabbit doll in 1903, registering the design at the Patent Office. She licensed wallpaper and created a board game, but died several years before Wedgwood brought out its line of Peter Rabbit dishes for young eaters in 1949.

What began as a most English country-garden tale is now a global phenomenon. Frederick Warne & Company licensed Peter's image in novel ways, and before me lies a Peter Rabbit pencil set made in China and labelled in Korean and English with 'The adventures of a naughty rabbit from Beatrix Potter's story-book' on the packaging. Next to it is 'The World Peter Rabbit' spoon and chopsticks gift set, now also sold online along with the Peter Rabbit baby line, including a potty seat and step stool. Peter Rabbit is available in 35 languages in 110 countries,[17] and for his 110th birthday, Pearson, the global publishing giant that long ago bought Frederick Warne, will publish a new rendition of Peter Rabbit, entitled *The Tale of a Naughty Little Rabbit*. They say that: 'There aren't many stories about naughty rabbits. That's because rabbits usually know how to behave themselves.'[18] We are not so sure . . .

While Pearson may advertise Peter as 'the most famous rabbit ever', Peter and his cousins were not the only rabbits frolicking on children's nursery ware. At her father's request, Sister Mary Barbara Vernon, daughter of Royal Doulton China's general manager, drew her designs for Bunnykins china by candlelight in her cloister. By 1937 there were 46 scenes available on children's two-handled cups and bowls. As a child I ate my porridge from a Bunnykins bowl, and for each of our children, we bought a Bunnykins mug. Where Peter Rabbit and his kin wore jackets and pinafores, Bunnykins bunnies were properly clothed, tricked out in dresses and suits, or even sporting lab coats or full armour. Bunnykins figurines went to school or the doctor's, they played musical instruments or golf, and they wore elaborate gowns or plus fours. The rabbits are us. What is it about these frolicsome and naughty bunnies, these bunnies in human dress, that so delights us? Why do bunnies serve to represent us so readily, whereas cats, dogs and horses fall short? It is Brer Rabbit who carries our hopes and fears against the fiercer, wilder creatures. However, he is wild himself, the dancer under the moon, the fiddler of the graveyards.

LUCKY RABBIT

Just as the person born in the Year of the Rabbit is lucky in business or gambling, Brer Rabbit is 'just born to luck'.[19] It makes sense, then, that a bit of that rabbit luck might wear off, particularly if you carry a rabbit's foot in your pocket. President Grover Cleveland was said to carry a rabbit's foot during the 1884 American presidential campaign, and his success was testimony to the power of the charm, or so an advertisement in Britain for imported American rabbit's feet would have its readers believe. The mascot on sale was also not just the foot of any old rabbit, but

> the left hind foot of a rabbit killed in a country graveyard
> at midnight, during the dark of the moon, on Friday the 13th
> of the month, by a cross-eyed, left-handed, red-headed
> bow-legged Negro riding a white horse.[20]

That was indeed a lucky rabbit's foot. It was from the sinister side of the bunny, and obtained in a graveyard during the dark of the moon, on an unlucky day by an unlucky man. Better still, the paw should be removed from the living rabbit, shot with a silver bullet. No wonder the cottontails became so wary, as Georgia's first poet laureate, Frank Lebby Stanton (1857–1927), understood:

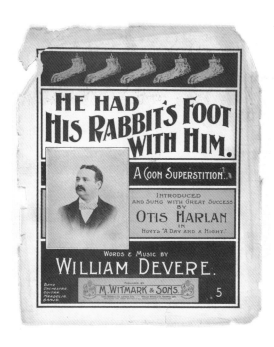

'He had His Rabbit's Foot with Him', sheet music, c. 1898.

In the white moonlight, where the willow waves,
He halfway gallops among the graves –
A tiny ghost in the gloom and gleam,
Content to dwell where the dead men dream,

But wary still!
For they plot him ill;
For the graveyard rabbit hath a charm
(May God defend us!) to shield from harm.
. . .
He holds their secret – he brings a boon
Where winds moan wild in the dark o' the moon;

Bavolet était le plus fier marin de Gascogne, avec ses poings robustes, il en remontrait à tous les boxeurs anglais.

Où qu'il se trouvait à terre, et un peu plus que de coutume, il arriva sur une grande place où l'on chauffait un superbe ballon.

Voilà mon loup de mer qui prétend que cette machine ne saurait s'élever et qui s'offre à monter dans la nacelle.

On accepte sa proposition, et Bavolet lui intérieure, commence à s'élever dans les airs, à sa grande stupéfaction.

Il monte, il monte toujours, tout à coup le ballon tourne sur lui même, et manque de renverser Bavolet qui se retient aux cordages.

Enfin le ballon éprouve une forte secousse, et Bavolet est tout étonné de se trouver dans un pays qu'il n'avait jamais vu.

La végétation était merveilleuse, les gâteaux poussaient comme des champignons, des bouteilles de liqueurs pendaient aux arbres.

Dans ce singulier pays, les poules tenaient les renards en laisse.

Les loups et les cerfs vivaient en bonne intelligence.

Ce pays était habité par des individus à tête de lapin et à pieds de bouc ce qui lui donnait un aspect très singulier.

Ces curieux habitants reçurent Bavolet avec beaucoup de civilités, et lui offrirent bon souper et bon lit.

Notre marin ne dormait jamais que d'un œil, bonne précaution, car la femme de son hôte venait à pas de loup pour l'assassiner.

Bavolet se redresse vivement saisit la traitresse au collet, l'entraîne dans sa tente et l'étrangle sans plus de façon.

Bavolet désenchanté, regarde tristement les débris de son ballon. Oh ! bonheur, le para chute est intact !

Il peut donc quitter cette terre inhospitalière et retourner dans son pays.

Il raconte ses aventures à son ami Maturon qui n'a assure qu'il n'aura jamais la curiosité de visiter cette singulière contrée.

Typ. Lith. Imagerie Raymond. Edit à Aubé à Mauzaison, Morette, Sque.

And gold shall glitter and love smile sweet
To whoever shall sever his furry feet![21]

What made people so eager to sever poor Rabbit's furry feet? The foot of a graveyard rabbit brought with it some of the power of that ghastly place, and the foot of a rabbit killed on the grave of an evil-doer was an especially powerful charm (President Cleveland's rabbit foot was supposedly taken on the grave of the outlaw Jesse James). A rabbit's foot might also stand in for the powerful fetish of a human bone, removed from an enemy or even a sorcerer. Carrying such a fetish gave the wearer not only good luck, but the power to resist malice and evil. For many African Americans in the twentieth century, the rabbit's foot charm partook of some of Brer Rabbit's guile, and helped the wearer resist the depredations of a discriminatory legal system.[22] Silver-mounted rabbits' feet were sold in quantity in New Orleans, and one scholar commented ironically that if all the talismans sold were what they said they were, 'the peace of many a rustic graveyard must have been broken by the midnight roar of artillery to supply the huge numbers of rabbit's [sic] feet these New Orleans jewelers have.'[23]

The New Orleans rabbit's foot merchants also found a ready market for their wares across the pond. In Britain bone amulets had a long history. Carrying the right foot of a rabbit was a sure remedy against lumbago and sciatica, while a rabbit bone could guard against toothache.[24] The last bone of the back of the rabbit was also a powerful charm, and a rabbit's foot was sometimes mounted in bonnets among unlucky peacock feathers.[25] Schoolchildren in Britain sitting exams would bring a rabbit's paw for luck, and on the first day of the month they would chant: 'White Rabbit, White Rabbit, White Rabbit' for luck all month long.[26]

While Brer Rabbit was cunning and unscrupulous, in European folklore rabbits could be positively evil. Rabbits were indeed

Aventures de Bavolet, 1860–70, lithograph. The French sailor Bavolet finds himself in an unknown land where he is attacked by a female rabbit, whom he strangles.

counted unlucky, and if a white rabbit crossed your path it was a token of death.[27] On no account could rabbits be eaten, brought aboard or even mentioned by British sailors, who refer to rabbits, when forced to mention them at all, as 'long-ears', 'furry thing' or 'bob-tailed bastards'.[28] A similar superstition prevailed in France, where mariners referred to 'big ears' (*grandes oreilles*), 'furry beast' (*bêtes à poils*) or simply 'the beast' (*la bête*). Considering the popularity of the rabbit as food and clothing in both cultures, the prohibition was startling, and surprisingly similar to the prohibition against women on board. Like woman, rabbit appears as both familiar domestic and wild shapeshifter. Witches often took the form of rabbits, and the severed paw of the witch-rabbit, which equated to a finger or hand, gave the wearer power over her. In 1930 a man visiting an elderly great-aunt in Devonshire remarked on the quantity of very dark rabbits in the fields. His great-aunt, a pillar of the Church, replied 'in a rather shocked voice, "But, my dear, nobody shoots those." I asked why, and she said, "Don't you really know the reason? They might be witches".'[29] If such a rabbit were shot, the witch would be known when she showed the same injury.

Witches were, of course, not necessarily old women; they could be young beauties. In a tale from North Carolina a young man's car breaks down and he knocks on the door of a rural house. He sees in the window 'a blue-eyed rabbit about three or four feet high . . . with human features'. The animal disappears and soon a beautiful young lady answers the door. A little time later she is found dead of gunshot wounds, shot by a silver bullet as she ran in her rabbit form.[30] Not all famous shape-shifting rabbits are women. Harvey, a six-foot three-and-a-half-inch tall white rabbit, is the eponymous if invisible presence in the 1950 James Stewart film of the same name. Stewart, who likes his drink a bit too much, has found an ideal companion in the rabbit-pooka.

The pooka, or púca, an Irish spirit, is more usually encountered in the shape of a dog or a pony that takes its victim on a wild ride. Harvey is a more gentle transatlantic sort, but he does indeed take those around him on a whimsical journey.

There is nothing whimsical, however, in the silent, fanged rabbit that beckons Donnie Darko on his strange, fantastical journey into time past or future in the 2001 film of the same name.

John Tenniel, illustration of Alice and the White Rabbit from *Alice's Adventures in Wonderland* (1865).

In Native American tales the rabbit is often a messenger and guide. In *Watership Down* Richard Adams used the 'Black Rabbit of Inlé' as the messenger of death. The Black Rabbit comes in the night and calls a rabbit by name and he must go: 'The Black Rabbit smelled as clean as last year's bones and . . . his eyes . . . were red with a light that gave no light.'[31]

The most famous white rabbit of all is also a messenger, beckoning Alice on her journey to Wonderland. He is an ordinary domestic variety of rabbit with pink eyes, except of course he is not mute, as household rabbits are, and he has both a waistcoat-pocket and a watch to take out of it. Alice follows the anxious and time-obsessed White Rabbit (who may represent the particular perils of being adult) down the rabbit hole. Though he does not shift his shape, Alice's Rabbit is variously herald, court clerk and steward; when Alice wakes he returns to being simply a large albino rabbit, though in that knowing red eye Lewis Carroll may have glimpsed the character of his famous literary creation, just as Beatrix Potter saw the inspiration for Peter Rabbit in a Belgian buck called Peter Piper 'bought at a very tender age, in the Uxbridge Road, Shepherd's Bush, for the exorbitant sum of 4/6'.[32]

Before me sits a wind-up metal toy. It is a white rabbit with pink eyes and white plastic ears, shaped like an egg and wearing a pink flower-sprigged waistcoat: an Easter rabbit made in China. While Easter is not much celebrated in Asia, it remains an important holiday in the West, bringing together rabbits and eggs (except of course in Australia, which celebrates with the Easter Bilby). The connection with egg-bearing rabbits seems to have begun in seventeenth-century Germany and is now widespread throughout Europe and North America. Twentieth-century Easter cards and postcards usually portray the Easter Bunny as a large male rabbit, often clothed like the White Rabbit in traditional European dress. These rabbits paint eggs, carry baskets, beat egg drums wearing a red 'Liberté' cap with a bandolier slung over one shoulder, conduct a rabbit chorus and, dressed in uniform, ride chickens. Rabbits, white and brown, also appear in more 'natural' poses, with a flock of chicken, guarding a nest of eggs or held precariously in a child's arms.

There are few female rabbits, who despite embodying the fertility associated with Easter, are evidently stay-at-home bunnies where egg delivery is concerned, with one important exception, *The Country Bunny and the Little Gold Shoes*. In 1939, DuBose Heyward, an American author and poet, and the librettist for Gershwin's popular opera *Porgy and Bess*, penned a story for his daughter Jennifer. A year later Heyward was dead, but his story outlived him, wonderfully illustrated by Marjorie Flack, an American children's book artist. Unlike Peter Rabbit, the 'little girl Cottontail' did not want to make mischief in someone else's garden. She wanted to be an Easter Bunny:

> There are really five Easter Bunnies, and they must be the five kindest, and swiftest, and wisest bunnies in the whole wide world, because between sunset on Easter Eve and dawn on Easter morning they do more work than most rabbits in a whole year.[33]

Her ambition scorned by the big, tough Jack Rabbits, and almost thwarted by her 21 babies, the Country Bunny nevertheless perseveres to realize her dream. She becomes not only the sole female Easter Bunny, but as she is wise, swift, kind and the bravest of all, she becomes the Gold Shoe Easter Bunny! For young girls growing up during and after the Second World War, the Country Bunny symbolized feminist aspiration, memorable for its depiction of the devoted and well-organized Mother Cottontail, and her triumph against odds. Still in print, and republished for the 70th anniversary in 2010, Heyward's gift to his daughter embodies the resilience of the tribe rabbit and mother:

Easter postcard, France, early 20th century.

> Because you have such a loving heart for children, I am going to give you the best but the hardest trip of all. Far off over two rivers and three mountains there is a great mountain peak. And in a little cottage on that peak is a

little boy who has been ill for a whole year, and who has been so brave that never once has he cried or complained. The mountain is so high that there is ice on the top, and it will be hard to climb, but if you get there you will give more happiness than any other Easter Bunny.

Cottontail picked up the egg very gently and went hopping away on her journey . . .[34]

Dressed in pinafores and waistcoats, coloured purple or pink, pounding rice endlessly, we bind rabbit to our service, yet rabbit, no matter how depicted or dismembered, remains apart, an emblem of the unknowable. What else is the magician's rabbit in the hat but an apparition from another world, a transmutation of nothing into something? Rabbit frequents our stories and our songs, but he remains a stranger to our species.

5   Rabbits and Us

There have been few more competent and objective observers of rabbits and their behaviours than the ethologist Ronald Lockley, yet he ends his monograph, *The Private Life of the Rabbit*, with these words: 'Rabbits are so human. Or is it the other way round – humans are so rabbit?'[1] We see in rabbits an echo of ourselves.

RABBITS AND THE MORAL LIFE OF CHILDREN

Lockley asks, 'Why does the rabbit amuse and charm us?' Is it the rabbit's 'baby face and whiskered charm', or is it 'their innocent, happy preoccupation with their simple way of living?'[2] Certainly the rabbit's soft, round form, domesticity and often endearing habits have encouraged its identification with both women and children, and in particular made them desirable pets for young girls and boys. The engraved frontispiece to Caleb Bement's treatise of 1859 on raising rabbits, *The Rabbit Fancier*, depicts a sweet young girl feeding leaves to a pretty doe and her brood of soft white bunnies. This image is echoed and repeated in countless sentimental portraits of children fondling and feeding hutch rabbits. Girls cradle rabbits in their arms, boys tentatively hold out a scrap of lettuce, though in one tableau by Richard Dadd, a nineteenth-century English artist (later incarcerated in an asylum for the murder of his father), a boy grabs a white rabbit by its ears

Frontisiece to
Caleb Bement,
The Rabbit Fancier
(1861 edition).

with less than gentle intent. The rabbit was a common accessory
for Victorian portrait painters, little girls being shown with small
bunnies, boys often with larger rabbits. As the British rabbit fancier
George Morant pointed out, 'they are all pretty objects'.[3] However,
rabbits were not just for cuddling. Almost all treatises on rabbits
echoed Bement's assurance to potential rabbit keepers that there
was 'a moral value attached to these animals'. Raising rabbits
taught responsibility at a young age, and supplied 'innocent and

Kitagawa
Utamaro, *Child
with Toy Rabbit*,
18th century,
woodcut.
A father holds
out a rabbit toy
to his infant son.

unfailing amusement'.[4] It was just such pleasant (and profitable) amusements that kept young people at home, and this was particularly important for boys, who were wont to turn their attention early to other pursuits:

This matter of rabbitry . . . many boys – for whose benefit they are chiefly introduced – and *men* even, may do worse than spend their time in such apparent trifles. It is even better than going to a horse-race. It is better even than going to a trotting match, where *fast men*, as well as fast horses, congregate.[5]

Rabbit raisers agreed, boys not only benefited from learning how to manage small livestock, but were deemed more capable of caring for animals, particularly in one specific area.[6] Little girls might be encouraged in rabbit feeding, but it was boys who could take on the more earthy business of breeding:

The adult bucks are overbearing, mischievous, and quarrel-some. Success very much depends on the way in which they are managed; and consequently, rabbit-keeping is an amusement better adapted for boys than for girls, unless, indeed, they have an elder brother or parent who will take upon himself the entire direction of the breed-ing department.[7]

Both boys and girls were encouraged to care for animals in their charge, but without sentimentality. Rabbit was considered a 'superior food' for children, and fortunately, 'children in par-ticular generally prefer him to beef and mutton'.[8] Rabbits were known to be 'dainty feeders', and what could be more appropriate than rabbit meat in the nursery, served on rabbit-strewn china plates? Once bunny had been boiled, braised or curried, his fur made soft muffs for tiny hands.

Picture books showing domestic and pet rabbits were popu-lar Victorian and Edwardian children's gifts, but imaginary rabbits also became central figures in stories specially written for children. The original Brer Rabbit tales are often not suitable for young ears, but Joel Chandler Harris used the device of the storyteller and the child to make them acceptable for families. The success of Brer Rabbit made rabbits central characters in the animal stories popular at the beginning of the twentieth century. Uncle Wiggily Longears was the protagonist of a series of books written by Howard R. Garis starting in 1906. In France in the 1920s, Benjamin Rabier populated his *bandes dessinées* ('drawn strips') with comic rabbits, cohorts of his most famous character Gédéon, the duck. Little Grey Rabbit was the main character in Alison Uttley's classic British children's series, begun in 1929 with *The Squirrel, the Hare and the Little Grey Rabbit*. And of course there is Rabbit, friend of Pooh and Christopher Robin in A. A. Milne's *Winnie-the-Pooh*, first published in 1926. Here, Rabbit is companion to a human child, as is *Pookie*, the rabbit with wings, who lives with his rescuer and caregiver Belinda, the Wood-cutter's daughter. Ivy Wallace began this sentimental series about the 'little white furry rabbit, with soft floppity ears, big blue eyes, and the most lovable rabbit smile in the world' in 1946, and my mother gave me my first Pookie book for my fifth birthday.[9]

These rabbit figures are actors in animal societies that mimic the human, with additional elements of the fantastical or fabulous (Uncle Wiggily has a hot-air balloon; Pookie consorts with goblins and elves). Toy rabbits were popular in nurseries, and they too could become treasured companions to children. The most famous story of bunny love is *The Velveteen Rabbit* by Margery Williams, first published in 1922 and echoed in a recent American children's book by Newberry Medalist Kate DiCamillo, *The Miraculous Journey of Edward Tulane* (2008). In both stories the toys undergo transformation as they are loved and abandoned and found again. In her famous 'bunny books' Beatrix Potter was, however, the first to identify the bunny with the child, clothing

60

Winnie-the-Pooh and Rabbit

a human character in rabbit fur.[10] Peter Rabbit exemplified the behaviour of a disobedient, if adorable, boy. He lost his shoes and his coat, he ate too much and he got into trouble by not listening to his mother. The little white rabbit in Margaret Wise Brown's *The Runaway Bunny* (1942) is equally naughty, threatening to run away from home, but his mother assures him that she will always come after him, the words every anxious child longs to hear: "'If you run away,' said his mother, 'I will run after you. For you are my little bunny.'"[11] In *Goodnight Moon*, written in 1947 by the same author, the wakeful 'child' is a bunny in striped pyjamas, and the 'quiet old lady who was whispering "hush"' is a large rabbit in a rocking chair.

If rabbits could become children, so could children act as rabbits, or at least this was the premise of Ernest Thompson Seton's *The Wild Animal Play for Children*. Seton described his best-selling book *Wild Animals I Have Known* as a collection of histories with a moral, and that moral was 'we and the beasts are kin'.[12] When he came to write his musical play he chose characters from his natural history, including Raggylug and his mother, Molly Cottontail. Molly is described as cute, wee and shy, a 'sweet

Molly Cottontail, from *The Wild Animal Play for Children* by Ernest Thompson Seton (1918).

little rabbit-girl in white', while Rags is 'a boy-rabbit larger than Molly'. Molly embodies the devoted mother rabbit:

> I set all my heart on my baby.
> For him I was bold in the strife;
> I taught him how wits may be stronger than strength.
> And loved him far more than my life.[13]

The animals enter the scene and tell their tales, but are terrified when the Sportsman (played by a 'big boy, with black whiskers') comes on stage. Fortunately, they are saved by the Angel of the Wild-things, who points her wand at the Sportsman and kills him. The Angel then praises the courage of all the animals, but it is the wee, shy Molly who is crowned Queen of the Wood:

> Then hail Molly Cottontail, Queen of the Woods!
> Her duty she did as she could;
> She died, so must all, but in triumph she died,
> So Molly is Queen of the Wood.[14]

Children could exemplify the rabbit virtues of love and duty, and in so doing triumph in life (though, as Seton noted, animal stories are all tragedies, since they always end in death).

Seton was not the only moralist who imagined children could be rabbits. One of the more unusual conflations of young boys and rabbits was created by Ervin S. Chapman, an earnest businessman and patriot, who authored *Particeps Criminis, The Story of a California Rabbit Drive* in 1910. Half natural history and half temperance sermon, Chapman used the device of the brutal and brutalizing rabbit drive as a metaphor for the effects of the 'demon liquor' on America's young manhood. His descriptions

and illustrations of the actual rabbit drive are disturbing even today. Once the rabbits realize they are trapped within the corrals to which they have been driven by the beaters,

> The merry twinkle of their eyes is gone and in its stead a glassy brilliancy of fear is seen. They rush from side to side of the enclosure . . . In vain they leap and bound and dash against each other and against the enclosing walls. Their efforts everywhere are unsuccessful. [15]

The drive ends badly for both rabbits and drivers:

> To each successful rabbit drive there is a tragic termination. The wild and terrifying tumult of the moving cordon ceases when the rabbits are all housed in the corral and the gate is closed by sturdy men crowding thickly into that narrow entrance. But when the men leap into the corral and with clubs savagely begin the work of beating them to death,

the helpless bunnies, like ten thousand weeping babies, cry and rend the air with wails of anguish until sometimes the most inveterate rabbit hater turns deadly pale and, trembling, quits the field. Only men of iron nerve can prosecute this cruel slaughter, and even such will sometimes, when the work is done, turn instantly and in silence hasten to their homes. Few who attend a rabbit drive desire ever to witness one again ... A gentleman of my acquaintance, when recently relating his attendance at a rabbit drive, solemnly and with much emphasis declared that he would end his own life rather than to witness such a scene again.[16]

If the rabbit drive is an example of such savage atrocity that it makes grown men turn pale, how much worse are the abuses inflicted on the male children of the nation:

The rabbit drive and the boy drive! The one illustrates the other. Some of their features are startlingly similar ... Twenty thousand bunnies slain during a few frolicsome hours! Twenty million boys diligently sought, for a far more savage slaughter ... Around that field the cordon of Satanic influences is extended. Over that field the boy drive is now in active operation, and from that field, where all is now so glad and gay, many will be borne to vagrancy and vice as the playful bunnies are driven from their joyous freedom to their awful doom.[17]

The title of this temperance tract, *Particeps criminis*, is the legal term for an accessory to a crime, and Chapman aims his book at parents, politicians, bartenders and liquor manufacturers, all those responsible for introducing the flower of America to alcohol and its attendant evils. Boys are like bunnies, playful, guileless and trusting, easy to herd down the unrighteous paths of drunkenness, where they fall, bludgeoned by despair and disease. If only those responsible could see the effects of their 'rabbit drive', they would turn from their sordid practices.

RABBITS IN LOVE

The rabbits of children's tales and moralizing stories are often poor, silly, weak things, at the mercy of adults both animal and human, who variously confine, harm or even slaughter them, though, like Molly, they can show surprising courage. However, there is another side to the rabbit, the dancer in the moonlight, that belies the nursery stories.

There is a story about how Ol' Brer Rabbit went courting, and he was not after does. Or at least that is what the illustrations to the first edition of Joel Chandler Harris's *Uncle Remus, His Songs and His Sayings* would suggest. Brer Rabbit and the other animals were always visiting 'Miss Meadows en de gals', but it was Brer Rabbit, who considered himself a bit of a ladies' man, who succeeded in marrying one of them, a certain Molly Cottontail.[18] Frederick Stuart Church, the illustrator of the *Uncle Remus* stories, did not, however, draw a bevy of charming whiskered rabbit beauties, but created dusky human nymphs in long white robes with flowers in their hair, who seem susceptible to Brer Rabbit's dubious charms. Ol' Brer Rabbit is not the only bunny to court interspecies. In 'The Rabbit's Bride' by the Brothers Grimm, the rabbit who raids the cabbage patch demands that the gardener's daughter sit upon his tail and come to his rabbit hutch. She resists but the third time she is asked, she falls for the persistent rabbit, and off she goes to the hutch to make the wedding feast:

Frederick Stuart Church, 'Miss Meadows and the Girls', illustration from Joel Chandler Harris, *Uncle Remus, His Songs and His Sayings* (1881).

All the hares came, and the crow who was to be the parson to marry them, and the fox for the clerk, and the altar was under the rainbow. But the maiden was sad, because she was so lonely.[19]

No wonder she was lonely – she was marrying not just out of clan or town, she was marrying ex-genera. She tricked the rabbit and ran home to her mother, and the rabbit was very sad. Rabbit–human unions do not usually work out well. In the animated film *Who Framed Roger Rabbit* (1988) the rabbit's bride also has no fur. Jessica Rabbit, Roger's voluptuous spouse ('I'm not bad, I'm just drawn that way'), professes her love for the goofy cartoon rabbit. What is it about rabbits?

Male rabbits do have a reputation for sexual athleticism, and the frenzy with which the buck exhibits his desire impresses many an observer. He will chase the doe round and round, leap over her, spray her with his scented urine, grunt and walk towards his intended stiff-legged, tail raised, taut with sexual energy. The sex act itself is brief, but the energy expended large, as Gervase Markham noted in the mid-seventeenth century in his self-help book, *A Way to Get Wealth*:

They are violently hot in the act of generation and perform it with such vigor and excess, that they swoon and lye in trances a good space after the deed is done.[20]

D. H. Lawrence, who wrote so intensely about passion both suppressed and consummated, used the buck rabbit as a device to express sexual tension between a man and a woman. In *Women in Love* (1920), Gudrun and Gerald, soon to become lovers, struggle with Bismarck, a large English rabbit, who lashes out in a fury when lifted from his hutch:

The long, demon-like beast lashed out again, spread on the air as if it were flying, looking something like a dragon, then closing up again, inconceivably powerful and explosive.

Gerald eventually subdues him, then releases him on the grass, where he and Gudrun watch the rabbit:

I'm not bad,
I'm just drawn
that way.

Jessica Rabbit from
*Who Framed Roger
Rabbit* (dir. Robert
Zemeckis, 1988).

'It's mad,' said Gudrun. 'It is most decidedly mad.'

He laughed.

'The question is,' he said, 'what is madness? I don't suppose it is rabbit-mad.'

'Don't you think it is?' she asked.

'No. That's what it is to be a rabbit.'

There was a queer, faint, obscene smile over his face. She looked at him and saw him, and knew that he was initiate as she was initiate. This thwarted her, and contravened her, for the moment.

'God be praised we aren't rabbits,' she said, in a high, shrill voice.

The smile intensified a little, on his face.

'Not rabbits?' he said, looking at her fixedly.

Slowly her face relaxed into a smile of obscene recognition.

'Ah Gerald,' she said, in a strong, slow, almost man-like way. 'All that, and more.' Her eyes looked up at him with shocking nonchalance.[21]

The violence and madness of the rabbit presage the ultimately disastrous relationship between Gudrun and Gerald. They are like rabbits, over-excited, over-sexed and doomed.

The unrepressed sexual desire of the buck is also expressed in his propensity to mate with almost any moving object, giving rise to myths about rabbits mating with cats or chickens (the origin of the Easter egg?).[22] Was it this lack of discretion that led to the famous case of Mary Toft? In September 1726 news reached London of the alleged birth of several rabbits to Mary Toft in Surrey. This extraordinary circumstance was reported to the court, and King George despatched his own physician to investigate the case. The gullible Dr André was convinced of the truth of Toft's assertion that she had one day been startled by a rabbit and gave chase to another:

> That same Night she dreamt she was in a Field with those two Rabbets in her Lap, and awakened with a sick Fit, which lasted till Morning; from that time, for above three months, she had a constant and strong desire to eat Rabbets, but being very poor and indigent cou'd not procure any.[23]

It was widely accepted at the time that if a woman while pregnant caught sight of an unusual animal, ate an unusual food or witnessed a strange incident, her unborn child might easily be affected. Strawberry birthmarks were evidently the result of eating strawberries. Given the rampant sexuality of the rabbit, there was no telling what might happen to a poor woman lusting after lagomorph. A broadsheet poem published about what soon became a scandal embellished Mary's brief report:

> The Rabbit all day long run in my Head,
> At night I dreamt I had him in my Bed;
> Methought he there a Burrough try'd to make
> His head I patted and I Strok'd his Back,
> My Husband wak'd me and Cry'd Moll for Shame
> Lett go – What 'twas he meant I need not Name.[24]

The 'rabbit' that Moll (remember Cottontail Molly) caressed may not have been an actual rabbit, as her husband suggested, and the 'Burrough' has perhaps another meaning.[25] Rabbits were called 'conies' and their name derived from the Latin *cuniculus*, which meant 'underground passage'. *Cuniculus* is very close to *cunnus*, the Latin term for female genitalia, and the rest is history. In seventeenth- and eighteenth-century English slang, men obsessed with sex were described as 'cunny-haunted', while those soliciting a prostitute were 'cunny hunters'.[26] In France, over-sexed men were called 'hot rabbits' (*lapins chauds*), while men accused of the sin of sodomy were said to refuse the *pel de conin* or rabbit fur. (Though in late Imperial China, homosexual men were called rabbits.) The link between *cunnus* and Latin *cuniculus*, French *conin* and English 'coney', meant that women were closely identified with rabbits. A woman judged to be overly productive was referred to as a 'rabbit-mother' or a *mère lapine*.[27] In a famous French ballad, the fifteenth-century poet Charles d'Orléans thanks his cousin for the gift of white rabbits (*blancs connins*), which may or may not have been actual furry bunnies.[28] In English, 'bunny' came to mean woman,[29] and in early twentieth-century Britain 'bun' could refer to a prostitute, while 'bunny' can also mean female sexual organs.

Most famously in the twentieth century, women were represented as highly sexualized Playboy Bunnies. Originally the 'Playboy' was identified with the male rabbit, chosen by magazine founder Hugh Hefner as the logo for his magazine because

William Hogarth, *Cunicularii; or, The Wise Men of Godliman in Consultation*, 1726, illustration depicting the story of Mary Toft.

'If you must be a dumb BUNNY stay one jump ahead of trouble!' American wartime poster warning against sexually transmitted diseases, showing a sailor bunny running towards a Prophylactic ('pro') Station, 1945.

rabbits appeared to like sex. The male rabbit logo continues to appear in popular culture from T-shirts to keychains. The Bunnies, however, were created in 1960 when Hefner was staffing his original Playboy Club in Chicago. Between 1960 and 1991, 25,000 women became Bunnies, part rabbit, part woman, a hybrid creature that evidently aroused in men what the sight of those lusty buck rabbits aroused in Mary Toft.[30]

The strong and long-standing association between rabbits and women in European popular culture may also account for the superstitions of French sailors who would not refer to the rabbit by name for fear of disaster at sea. Bringing rabbits or

'Six British Girls Who are to Leave London to Train as Bunny Girls at the Headquarters of Playboy Clubs in Chicago USA', *Playboy* (14 October 1965).

women on a ship might lead to uncontrolled reproduction and the ship and its bunny-fearing crew would be lost.

This identification of women and rabbits in European culture made the rabbit itself a cipher for the qualities of particular women, especially those iconic females who represented love, motherhood and fertility. Since classical times, hares had been emblematic of lust, fecundity and a strange ambiguous sexuality. For the Greeks, this made the hare the most appropriate sacrifice to Aphrodite, since she possessed the gift of fertility to a superlative degree.[31]

By the Renaissance, as the domestic rabbit spread throughout Europe, artists began to picture the common rabbit of house and garden as the symbol both of sensual pleasure and of motherhood and rebirth. In a marvellous fifteenth-century fresco showing Venus triumphant over Mars (love over war), the goddess sits on a throne drawn by two white swans, and on the shores gambol white rabbits, now become her emblem. In Piero di Cosimo's sixteenth-century painting of a recumbent Venus, a large white rabbit presses against the smooth rosy flesh of the goddess of love, nuzzling her thigh next to the infant Cupid. In a later, less mythological age, the artist Rosalba Carriera (1675–1757) depicted a young woman *en déshabillé*, cuddling a soft bunny against her breast, an allusion to Venus, and perhaps to the practice of medieval nuns who were chastised for bringing their rabbits to church, snuggled under their habits. More disturbing perhaps is Mark Ryden's twenty-first-century depiction of a pubescent Sophia (wisdom) suckling a pink bunny in the presence of Jesus holding a Lamb of God. For Ryden, the bunny is emblematic of the world of childhood, of the imagination that infuses the inanimate with life, and in his painting the rabbit of imagination receives the milk of knowledge, an uncomfortable and uncanny thought.[32]

L'HEUREUX LAPIN.

Rabbits as symbols of Venus become themselves love tokens. Charles d'Orléans may have jested about *conins* and women, but in tapestries and illuminated manuscripts rabbits frolic in the garden of love. White rabbits play at the feet of the lovers in a fifteenth-century French tapestry, the 'Offering of the heart'. Most famously, they accompany the lady of the Unicorn tapestries, while in the *Histoire d'amour sans paroles* ('History of Love without Words'), a fifteenth-century illuminated manuscript that recounts

Hans Baldung Grien, *The Holy Family with St Anne and St Joachim*, 1510–11, woodcut.

the story of Jean de Brosse and his wife Louise de Laval, men and women play with rabbits in their burrows, an exchange freighted with symbolic meaning.

Not all these playful love rabbits are so innocent. White rabbits appear in Susanna's garden as she emerges from the bath, a symbolic reference to the unwelcome advances of the lecherous elders. Rabbits also appear in the original Garden, mute and hunched at the foot of Eve as she reaches for the apple of knowledge. In early sixteenth-century engravings such as Hans Baldung Grien's *The Fall of Man*, and Albrecht Dürer's famous image of Adam and Eve of 1501, or in Bosch's *Garden of Earthly Delights*, the rabbits (or are they the preternatural and lustful hares?) turn their backs, presenting their posteriors to the viewer, a blatant sign of animal desire, now about to enter the world. Eve will be a rabbit, and Adam cunny-haunted.

A century later the single white rabbit in Rubens's luscious Eden or the charming brown-and-white rabbits of a baroque Garden seem less menacing, allusions to the first Mother rather than to the Fall. Eve's scornful rabbit-hares are transformed into the gentle companions of her Virgin daughter. Renaissance artists seated the rabbit next to Mary, as a sign of grace and fertility, and surprisingly, virgin birth. Classical authors had thought the hare

Titian, *The Virgin of the Rabbit*, c. 1530.

a hermaphrodite, capable of self-impregnation, and thus an appropriate symbol of immaculate conception. The rabbit inherits this role. Baldung Grien populates his engraving of the Holy Family with playful bunnies that wash their ears, greet one another and even aid the artist, holding up the medallion with his initials. In his painting of the birth of the Virgin, Vittore Carpaccio depicts two household rabbits nibbling a cabbage leaf and very much at home at the entrance to the bedroom, signs of Virgin fertility to come. Titian places the white rabbit of innocence beneath Mary's outstretched hand, both as a companion and as a symbol of her purity, her fertility and her immaculate conception.[33]

THE RABBIT IN THE ROCKS

Who are these other brown rabbits in their burrows staring up at nativities and the transfigurations of saints? Why do they scamper knowingly up the steep paths of the gardens of Gethsemane as Christ prays? These are not placid hutch or courtyard rabbits, fed and petted by their keepers. In European paintings of the Renaissance and Baroque, these wild rabbits have a very different meaning from that of the white rabbits of fertility and virginity. In the Bible, Proverbs 30, Verse 26 was translated as 'The conies are but a feeble folk, yet make they their houses in the rocks'. There are no conies in the Holy Land (only hyraxes), but St Jerome, the great biblical translator, equated the hyrax with the common rabbit, then extrapolated to Moses, who when he fled Egypt, was like 'the little rabbit of the Lord'. Here, is the little rabbit peeking out of his burrow at the Nativity as painted by Girolamo dai Libri, and is St John the Baptist pointing to the newborn babe, or is he smiling at the rabbit, the signifier of Moses, the link with the Old Testament? In Bellini's masterpiece depicting St Francis in the wilderness, the rabbit, almost hidden in the rocks, is very much the little rabbit of the Lord, witnessing the ecstasy of the saint. However, the rabbits that scamper up the steep paths of the sombre garden of Gethsemane have another meaning. In medieval bestiaries the hare, now transformed into the rabbit, runs swiftly uphill to escape pursuers; so, too, the righteous when fleeing temptation might ascend to God.

WARRIOR RABBIT

Brer Rabbit is more interested in making love, not war, but as Lockley noted in his studies, both male and female will fight to defend their territories and their honour, or at least their right to a mate. He describes a fight between Big Boss and Bold Benjamin for dominance in the warren:

> They had met somewhere below. There was a thudding noise and they emerged together, rolling on the bare grass in a confused clinch. Separating, they leaped or pranced around each other for a few seconds . . . Then Benjamin darted in, bowling Boss over sideways, and sinking chisel-teeth into the neck.[34]

Lockley's descriptions fuelled the imagination of Richard Adams when he created the rabbit cultures of *Watership Down*: Hazel the natural leader; BigWig, the loyal subordinate, teeth and claws at the ready; Campion and Holly of the Owsla, the elite guard; and of course General Woundwort, still used by rabbit mothers as the bogeyman to subdue naughty bunnies. Adams's story revolves around male camaraderie, courage and individual daring, familiar in numerous books or films about men at war. The company of bucks is content in its hilltop stronghold, until a little bird (Kehaar, the wounded gull) tells them to seek out does

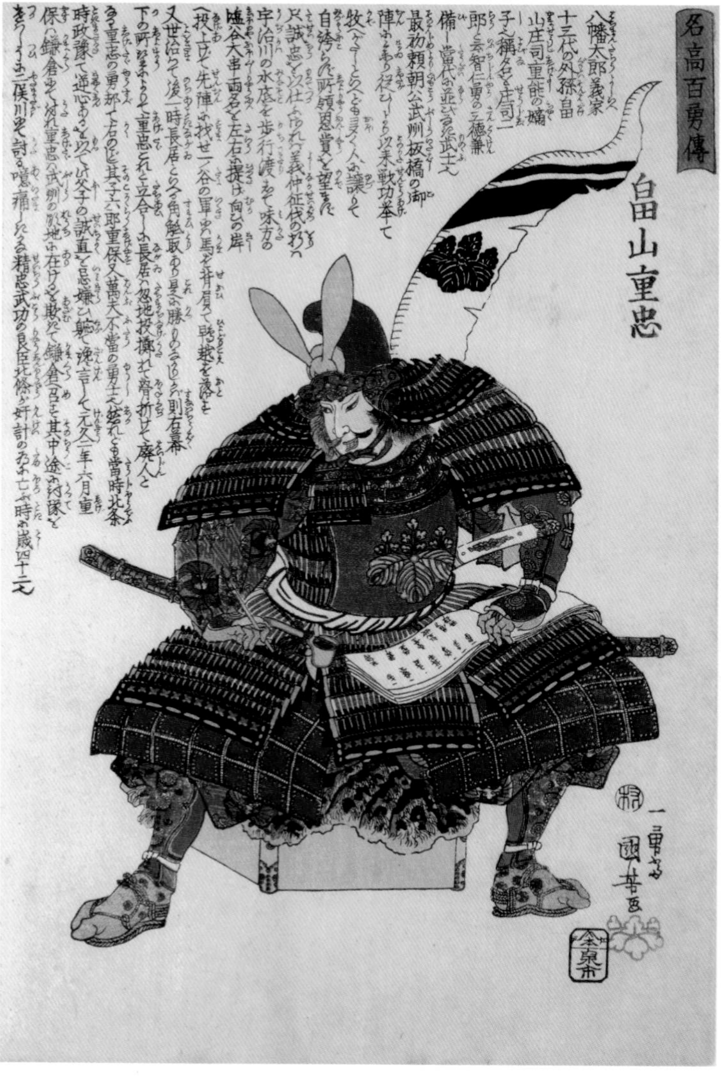

畠山重忠

八幡太郎義家
十二代の外孫畠
山庄司重能の嫡
子之稱名を庄司
次郎と云智仁勇の三德兼
備へ漢の近公宋の岳武王
最初賴朝公武州板橋の御
陣に加り又々父の人に讓り
牧（まきし）人又三人人讓り
自身は所領恩賞を望まず
只誠忠父心は仲代の打
宇治川の水庭を歩行渡して味方の庠
を進せて先懷に找せ一谷の平打は馬を肯負して駿駆を通じ
（投じ）て先陣に找せ一谷の平打は馬を肯負して駿駆を通じ
又世治に後一時長居しも魚鑑取の星も勝のえうたゝ則在希
下の所なりとする一重忠と立つて一の長居に忍地投擲れて磨折
多く重忠の勇新て右の如重忠保久黄六不當の勇士と松れるも前時北条
時政讓て述れと子右の如重忠保久黄六不當の勇士と松れるも前時北条
保へうるに深川老詩の噫補。稱。へる粘忠武功の良臣北榕が奸計のわ七兵時も歳四十二

to perpetuate the colony. Through raids on hutches and the burrows of others, they acquire mates, and the warriors of Watership Down cease from fighting and settle into domestic life.

Adams's book succeeds so well not only because he uses familiar human themes skillfully, but because he portrays the dangers, stratagems and struggles through 'rabbit' eyes, allowing readers that long-desired glimpse into the secret life of the hedgerow. Similarly, Ernest Thompson Seton used the story of a single mother struggling to raise her child against many odds as the core of his tale of RaggyLug, which he nevertheless maintained was a 'true story' of rabbit life, based on his field observations. Molly Cottontail taught her son all she knew about escape and trickery in a rabbit world, and showed the courage of her sex when she took on the snake in defence of her child.

The rabbit's noble character is also part of twentieth-century popular culture. *Crusader Rabbit*, the first animated series produced for television, premiered in 1950. Crusader is not a trickster, no Bugs Bunny or Brer Rabbit, using wits and cunning to defeat or humiliate his enemies; rather, each episode begins with the title sequence showing Crusader as a mounted knight galloping off to face the enemy. With the cowardly tiger, Rags, this Don Quixote of rabbits first heads to Texas to defend his own kind threatened with a rabbit drive, then takes on the causes of other species, or damsels in distress. *Usagi Yojimbo* ('Rabbit Bodyguard') is the saga of an equally courageous rabbit, ears tied in a classic samurai topknot. Miyamoto Usagi, created by Stan Sakai, an American cartoonist, embodies the virtues of Japanese ronin.[35] Usagi's skills as a warrior, his honour and his sense of mischief make him an apt companion for Hazel or BigWig.

Utagawa Kuniyoshi, *Hatakeyama Shigetada, Samurai, with Rabbit Ears on His Helmet*, 1843–4, woodblock print.

Die Vivisektion des Menschen.

Professor Karnickulus: Nur keine falsche Sentimentalität! Das Prinzip der freien Forschung verlangt es, daß ich diesen Menschen viviseziere zum Heile der gesamten Tierwelt!

We feel a certain thrill, a frisson of expectation, when the prey stops, turns and confronts the predator. Rabbit has been characterized as delicate, timid, gentle, confused, but he turns and presents a different face, aggressive, furious, fierce. This is witch rabbit, symbol of the uncanny, the reversal of the natural order of things. We laugh and then we shiver. Will the creature that we dominate so easily, whose neck we break with a casual twist and whose feet we wear for luck, stop, look us in the eye and go for the throat?

That is of course precisely what the Killer Rabbit of Caerbannogh does in the film *Monty Python and the Holy Grail* (1975). The Pythons understood well the humour in the situation where the underdog defeats the overweening enemy. A 'wee rabbit', what kind of threat can that be? One decapitated knight later it is evident that the rumours were true, and it takes the Holy Hand Grenade of Antioch to subdue the vicious killer bunny. While not a killer per se, Bunnicula, the title character of a children's book series by American author James Howe, is a vampire rabbit who bleeds vegetables to pallid death. Though the cat fears for the safety of the human household, Bunnicula, sporting fearsome teeth and glowing red eyes, is of gentle disposition. The same might not be implied of other fanged rabbits whose images populate the Internet. These are rabbits that seem perfectly capable of turning on their human foes. This reversal of the order of things has been an important theme in human–animal relationships, from the medieval illustrations of the human-sized hare harrying the hunter, to the giant mutant rabbits who turn against Australians in *The Year of the Angry Rabbit*, a science-fiction novel from 1964 by Russell Braddon. Originally a satire, Braddon's novel was turned into a kind of mutant carrot horror movie, *The Night of the Lepus*

The tables turned: a rabbit physician announces: 'Now no phoney sentimentality! The principle of free research requires that I vivisect this human for the health of the entire animal world.' From the German satirical magazine *Lustige Blätter*, Berlin, 1910.

(1972), now a cult film for both its strange premise and stilted acting and direction. While the idea of a giant killer rabbit makes us laugh, it also makes us pause: what if the strong and lusty rabbits turned against us? We have perpetrated such crimes against their kind. Would they show us mercy?

6 The Twenty-first-century Rabbit Paradox

'The rabbit always finds itself in paradoxical situations. Domesticated yet still wild, and a stay-at-home that's running around all over the world. In addition, it's both a pet and a lab animal. It's farmed for its meat but also for its fur, and it's also a therapeutic animal. The rabbit's modes of existence are as varied as they are heterogeneous', so say Catherine Mougenot and Lucienne Strivay, authors of *Man's Worst Friend* (2011).[1] We may pet them, draw them and treat them as members of the family, but at the same time their evident distance from the human species allows us to mutilate and murder them with scant regard for our shared 'humanity'.

RABBITS TO EAT

In the 1970s, the Rodale Press published a number of books designed to reacquaint 'back-to-the-landers' and newly minted organic farmers in the United States with the skills of their forebears. *Raising Rabbits* included chapters on such homey topics as 'Slaughtering and Dressing', 'Pelts' and 'Rabbit Meat Recipes'. Where rabbit meat had been a staple of the American working class diet in the early part of the twentieth century, its popularity then waned until the Second World War. With a shortage of beef for American tables, the United States Government published helpful pamphlets with titles like *Domestic Rabbits in the Food for Freedom Program*, and *Recipes for Cooking Domestic Rabbit Meat*. According to *Life* magazine in 1943, raising the 'friendly and decorative' creatures became a 'patriotic hobby'. Proponents urged Americans to establish backyard rabbitries for household use and for profit: 'Since Bunny can help mightily to buy the bungalow in the country later on, [the rabbit business] is a good start toward . . . economic independence.'[2]

Despite this official encouragement, American commercial rabbitries have remained small operations in comparison to their European counterparts, reflecting the larger traditional consumption of rabbit meat in France, Germany and other countries. For example, some American meat rabbit breeders consider sales of 500 rabbits a week a wild success. (Chefs refer to the 'Peter Rabbit syndrome' or 'Easter Bunny syndrome' to explain Americans' reluctance to embrace rabbit meat as a staple dish. Perhaps if it were called 'lapine'?[3])

In the 1950s, the large New Zealand and California white rabbits were introduced to commercial operations in France and Italy, and the European rabbit industry began to move from traditional household rearing to large-scale 'rational' rabbit production.[4] Today, some commercial operations in European countries house up to 10,000 does, and the relationship between bunny and breeder has irrevocably changed. Where once children fed their charges on cabbage leaves and kitchen scraps, rabbit raising has become not only rational but scientific, the seemingly inevitable approach to livestock rearing on an industrial scale.[5] The World Rabbit Science Association (WRSA) held its first general meeting in Dijon, France, in 1976, where the delegates no doubt dined on the traditional dish, *Lapin à la moutarde*. In addition to research on rabbit breeding, diseases and rational care, organizations such as the WRSA and UNESCO encourage the raising of rabbits as a high-quality food source in developing nations. Rabbits have always been touted as the poor man's panacea, guaranteeing economic independence for the small farmer in 1920s America, environmentally conscious husbandry for disaffected back-to-the-landers in the 1970s and now as an answer to demand for protein in Africa, Southeast Asia and the Caribbean. The renewable rabbit has become the twenty-first-century answer to global food security:

> In the wake of the worsening global economy, the spread of Avian Influenza, and the deterioration of our planet's natural resources, the role of the rabbit – to provide a regular supply of high quality protein and income – under sustainable systems that utilize renewable resources at

Rabbits behind a restaurant, China.

Guanhu Rabbit Industry Company, the largest rabbit farm in China.

minimal costs, is presently recognized as a major livestock species in many parts of the world.[6]

The European rabbit's intolerance for high temperatures has limited its natural spread, but the WRSA has pioneered rabbit-raising projects in Ghana, Haiti, El Salvador and Kenya. In China, international aid agencies also promote rabbit raising as a supplement to poor farmers' income, and China's 'Rabbit King' credits his success to the donation of a pair of rabbits in 1980.[7] The Chinese have been breeding European rabbits for food and fur for generations, and now China both produces and exports the largest number of rabbits worldwide, the bulk of production still raised in backyard rabbitries.[8] The European Union banned Chinese rabbit meat in 2002 due to concerns over high levels of contaminants, but rescinded the ban in 2004, in time for the expansion of Kangda Foods's rabbit business. This Chinese food manufacturing and processing group has recently built entire 'rabbit villages', where hundreds of thousands of white rabbits (and not the Jade Moon Rabbit) are raised in a most rational manner, to be shipped frozen to Europe, or packaged in frozen noodle dishes for the Asian market.[9]

This new rabbit industry comes at a cost, most specifically to the livestock. The decrease in diversity (the feet of old breeds cannot tolerate the wire-mesh floors of battery cages), the increase in communicable diseases and their prevention through pharmaceutical intervention, and the intensification of breeding regimes demanded in rational rabbit raising have not been welcomed by the rabbits. Animal rights activists have investigated battery rabbit farms as well as backyard operations, and in both the life of the meat rabbit is short and stressful. Like chickens, rabbits in intensive operations are crammed into small cages with little space for movement. They suffer from disease, boredom and sometimes ill treatment.[10] While does do breed several times per year in the wild, on farms they are forced to bear from six to twelve times a year, and end their short, joyless lives in exhaustion, many having never even been 'serviced' by a buck, since artificial insemination has replaced the too-messy business of mating. Their ending can also be painful and terrifying, as inexperienced raisers continue to use medieval killing methods, breaking the rabbits' necks or clubbing them between the ears with shortened, sawn-off baseball bats. Even in commercial rabbitries, the animals often die screaming; one American slaughterhouse planned to capitalize on bunny's last moments by selling the recorded death squeals to hunters to attract predator animals.[11]

In North America, since rabbit meat production is still perceived as a 'backyard industry', there has been little attempt at regulation, and rabbitries and rabbit meat are not subject to mandatory inspection by authorities. The animal rights movement has had an impact on the industry, and some rabbitries in the United States have been shut down, while in certain jurisdictions in Canada, where the industry is very small and limited to the traditional rabbit-eating province of Quebec and the Mediterranean-origin rabbit lovers of Ontario, growers are seeking to establish codes of best practice. The Australians, whose love–hate relationship with bunnies is legendary, wrote *A Code of Practice for the Intensive Husbandry of Rabbits* in 1991, to ensure stress-free environments in commercial rabbitries, though the Code specifically states that it 'does not include any consideration of the management of the European wild rabbit', whose welfare is most definitely not protected.[12]

RABBITS TO WEAR

The more successful the meat industry, the greater the problem of the by-products, and in particular the fur. Meat rabbits are often killed too young to produce good-quality pelts. In the past shaved fur and trimmings (feet, tail and ears) found uses as varied as felting, pillow stuffing, decorative trims and fertilizer, to say nothing of lucky rabbits' feet. While indifferent pelts are still being shipped from the slaughterhouses to fur 'dressers' (many located in China), good-quality pelts are destined for the fashion trade, where fur saw a resurgence in the 1990s. Rabbit fur is still a very minor part of the world fur trade, and the International Fur Trade Federation does not even include it in its description of furs either wild or farmed (and it does include coyote, North American squirrel, Chinese weasel and New

Zealand opossum). Its minor role cannot be attributed to the quantity of pelts being produced as a result of meat production and specialized fur-rabbit farming. One Italian company recorded sending between 60,000 and 200,000 frozen pelts a week to the Chinese fur dressers, and the Coalition to Abolish the Fur Trade estimates that tens to hundreds of millions of pelts are produced annually.[13]

White rabbit fur was once the most desirable, since it could be dyed and cut to imitate other, more expensive furs, but now with an over-supply of pelts from the meaty New Zealand and California whites, the market has turned to specialty fur breeds. Where the chinchilla rabbit was once the most desirable bunny in the 1920s (one breeder wrote that 'no fur could be more attractive'[14]), the Orylag (or Rex de Poitou), a French breed developed in 1985, is now the darling of the fashion industry, supplying houses such as Fendi, Dior, Chanel and Hermès with soft, dense fur. Fifteen years of research by French scientists at the Institut National de la Recherche Agronomique (INRA, National Institute for Agricultural Research) produced this new rabbit breed 'created to create'. The Orylag has no identity as rabbit; it is only fur. Beginning with the Rex, the most widely raised fur rabbit, the breeders crossed, selected and crossed again until they perfected the Orylag: 'You dreamed of a perfect material, we have invented it.' The rabbit is described as 'material', existing to be cut, shaped, assembled and worn, or to be made into soft plush bears and bunnies trademarked *Caresses d'orylag*, each sold with a certificate of authentication. Orylag is the perfect twenty-first-century product, 'the fruit of controlled scientific progress' that provides the seductive thrill of wearing the skin of another, but in 'a new ecological balance'. No wild animals were destroyed in the making of this coat, just Orylags.[15]

The Rex also originated in France, but at Nature's whim. The Rex is the result of a genetic mutation first seen in wild rabbits at the end of the First World War. The Rex mutation also occurs in rats and cats, but only in rabbits does it produce such an even dense and velvety coat. While Rex, Orylag and chinchilla fur may be recognizable as derived from a living animal, the fashion-fur industry transforms even poor pelts into everything from fuzzy pompoms and 'rabbit fur pectorals' to princess caps and berets. Knitted rabbit-fur scarfs, vests and jackets echo the aboriginal practice of weaving strips of fur to make warm garments. Despite natural abundance, the industry also offers fake rabbit fur (85 per cent polyester, 15 per cent acrylic), sometimes disguised as leopard:

> Imitation rabbit has a fashionable design, You're feeling uncharacteristically extravagant. They are lustrous in color . . . warm and comfortable to wear.[16]

The rabbit disguised as leopard, the prey sporting the colours of the predator, is as unnatural as the rabbit-fur flowers for sale in pink, yellow and green, and the charming purple rabbit-fur shawl.

The fur required for these novel creations is the product of carcasses, but there is another way to wear rabbit. Angora 'wool' is harvested from the living animal. Like sheep, angora rabbits are shorn, combed or, in the case of less lucky animals, plucked. In the 1920s, aristocratic British breeders such as Lady Rachel Byng were promoting the 'industry of Angora rabbit wool farming' as a 'God-send' to the unemployed. They avowed that the angora business was particularly suitable for women, since 'no killing is entailed'. Ladies could pet and pluck their rabbits with sure knowledge that they were not obliged to snap their necks. Lady Byng recommended beginning with 'an original stud' of two bucks, and four or five does, and thanks to their surprising reproductive rate, 'a farm of many hundred can be built up in two years'.[17] Angora farming remains a small-scale business, and in both France and China, the two largest centres of production, about 500 adult rabbits per operator or family is the norm. France was once the centre of the industry, but China now supplies almost all the world's product, having selectively bred its very own 'Chinese coarse wool Angora' in the 1980s.[18]

Angoras might be supposed to have a better quality of life
than than their meat cousins, since to produce superior wool the
rabbits must be raised individually in clean cages, and regularly
groomed. While the rabbits undoubtedly appreciate more com-
modious cages, they have little say on their grooming preferences.
The French 'pluck' their rabbits, having first provided them with
a supplement of Lagodendron, a depilatory fodder that loosens
the fur. French bunnies are sometimes left with a line of long fur
along their spines to keep them warm. Some farms shear rabbits
as if they were tiny sheep, and in New Zealand angora shearing is
a tourist attraction. The Chinese prefer to cut their rabbits' hair
and angora cutting has become a specialized trade. Angora yarn
is warm, soft and silky, and the long guard hairs give knitted

products their characteristic furry 'bloom'. Wearing angora next to the skin is like snuggling up to a warm and silky bunny, the desire of every child who ever sported a pair of coveted white angora mittens in a northern winter.

RABBITS TO SHOW

The angora is one of the 'fanciest' rabbits. Not just fancy in its looks, it is a rabbit that has captured the 'fancy' of breeders since the Victorian Age, when 'fanciers' exhibited their top animals with others who shared their tastes. Charles Darwin himself bred pigeons, and evidently frequented the company of rabbit fanciers. How else would he have known that a prize English lop weighed in at 18 lb (8 kg; wild rabbits average 3.25 lb, or 1.5 kg) with ears measuring 23.25 in (60 cm) from tip to tip, compared with the modest 7.5-in (20-cm) rack of the wild rabbit? The owner, 'a rabbit fancier of thirty years standing', had this magnificent specimen preserved in a glass case for perpetual exhibition.[19] Competition for prizes among fanciers was fierce, and winning rabbits were jealously guarded, their stud books kept as meticulously as those of race horses.

Lest one assume that the passion for unusual animals and their display is but a Victorian folly, it is salutary to examine the website of today's British Rabbit Council (BRC, heir to the British Rabbit Society and the National Rabbit Council of Great Britain and her Dominions). The BRC publishes a Breed Standards book and recognizes over 50 breeds and 500 varieties, some with lovely names, like the Giant Papillon, the Harlequin, the Blanc de Bouscat and the Wheaten Lynx.[20] The French, eager to claim their own, have special clubs devoted to the Fauve de Bourgogne, an ancient lineage first described in 1919 from the region of Burgundy, home of the celebrated *Lapin à la moutarde de Dijon*.[21] The American

Rabbit Breeders Association, or ARBA, was founded in 1925, though specialist clubs like the National Belgian Hare Club date to the late nineteenth century. Even the Australians have their fancy rabbit clubs, though much more recently established, given their rabbit history. The South Australian Rabbit Fanciers Society Inc (TSARFS) was founded in 2006 and 'aims to promote all aspects of our hobby in a friendly, family atmosphere'. TSARFS particularly welcomes the participation of 'young members' since they 'are the future of the fancy, and must be encouraged'.

The future of the fancy is, however, less likely to lie in the meat-pen displays and breed shows than on Facebook (see 'Fancy Rabbits Pakistan') and YouTube. While dogs and cats dominate the ratings, rabbits have moved into star category with clips of Champis, the Danish sheep-herding rabbit, the real Energizer bunny and baby bunnies snuggling.[22] Both the BRC and ARBA encourage young people to join, for rabbit breeding and showing not only foster '*critical thinking*' but are '*character-building youth activities*' (their emphasis).[23] Rabbits will keep young men and women off the mean streets of the twenty-first century as they kept them from the questionable pursuits of the nineteenth. They might, however, lure them to the dessage ring.

Rabbits have always hopped on their own, but with a little help from their owners they are leaping to unheard of heights. Rabbit jumping, while not yet an Olympic sport, has its devotees. Rabbit show jumping or dressage began in the 1970s in Scandinavia, where there are currently 50 clubs. Popularized first on television and now on YouTube, where the Danish Rabbit Show Jumping Championships feature the prodigious leaping feats of rabbits like Yaboo and the aptly named Lamborghini Gallardo, *kaninhop* has spread to North America, with the founding of the American Association of Sporting Events for Rabbits in 2009. There are clubs as well in Australia, Canada and Japan. The Australians (TSARFS) have patterned their meets after European competitions, but in a 'safe version', assuring prospective competitors both rabbit and human, that 'This rabbit sport promotes a healthy and happy rabbit and owner bonding experience.'[24] The Canadian Rabbit Hopping Club grew out of a project by two young Albertans as part of the 4-H youth organization, who have since participated in demonstrations at the Calgary Stampede (bunnies and broncos)

Snoopy jumps! Kaninhop Club, Jena, Germany, April 2011.

Grand Champion
Rabbit Fryer,
Coshocton County
Fair, Ohio, 2011.

and Bunanza 2012. One Danish enthusiast has online advice for
the novice human trainer:

> To calm or encourage your rabbit it is important, that you
> talk with your rabbit the whole time both at training and
> at events. Don't tell it off, if it doesn't go like you want . . .
> It is hard to say, if it is best to hop with a male or a female.
> We have had best luck with the females. Our males are often
> more interested in sniffing and peeing and mating our legs
> . . . Rabbit hopping is fun for children and grown ups, and
> it is a different good and exciting way to have rabbits and
> to be a rabbit.[25]

Rabbit hopping does indeed allow rabbits to be rabbits, even if
they are sometimes constrained by harnesses. It is less likely,
however, that rabbits enjoy their exhibition in the 'meat pen'
or 'fryer' categories at agricultural fairs. There is often little

room for sentimentality in the pen or show ring, as evident in a photograph of the champion rabbit of 1919, Prince Stanhope, whose father, Prince Leo, can be seen immortalized in the stole draped around the shoulders of his owner.

RABBITS TO TEST

Despite their being such 'pretty animals', researchers have displayed remarkably little sentiment for the welfare of the long-eared participants of countless experiments over the last 200 years. Beginning in the early 1800s, rabbits became the model of choice in rabies experiments, since they exhibited a form of the disease that resulted in paralysis, rather than slavering frenzy. Louis Pasteur, the great nineteenth-century French microbiologist, injected the rabies virus into rabbits' brains. They died, then he dried their spinal cords in an effort to attenuate or weaken the virus, so that it could serve as a vaccine against the disease in human subjects.

The European rabbit proved to be an excellent laboratory animal. Small, relatively docile, rapidly reproducing, easily restrained and rarely moaning, rabbits make work easier for researchers. Their well-veined, translucent ears make it simple for handlers to inject drugs or draw blood; their protruding eyes with thin corneas and no tear ducts allow clear observation of the effects of pathogens and chemicals; their skin, once shaved, is sensitive and easy to paint with toxins. So close to the human are aspects of rabbit physiology that they can be used in our place for uncomfortable, and in the case of the rabbit, sometimes fatal tests. First developed in 1927, the 'rabbit test' was used to determine pregnancy in human females. Injection of the urine of a pregnant human female engenders changes in the ovaries of a female rabbit. Unfortunately, in order to observe this change, the doe must be killed and dissected. Fortunately, new pregnancy tests have saved many rabbits from being used to reveal a condition that by its nature becomes quickly self-evident.[26]

The rabbit's baby-like face and its association with children and innocence have served to make it the poster animal for cruelty-free products. For many people images of weeping, scarred bunnies arouse indignation and a deep revulsion against human indifference to the suffering of others, particularly for the cosmetic fripperies of life. Organizations such as People for the Ethical Treatment of Animals (PETA), My Beauty Bunny, Leaping Bunny and Choose Cruelty Free all sport bunny logos, and the Humane Society International features white rabbits in its 2012 campaign to end animal testing. In 2010 PETA also developed a 'bunny' app for the iPhone that used two kinds of bunny to make its point.[27] Their efforts and those of animal rights groups have turned the tide against cosmetic testing on rabbits, but rabbits continue to be used as research subjects for medical interventions and drug testing.[28] Again, their physiological similarity in some areas has made them subjects for infection with human

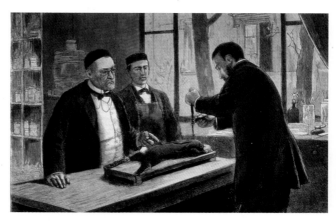

The French chemist M. Pasteur experiments on a chloroformed rabbit', 1885.

Will Crawford,
'Vivisection',
Puck, 1911. 'The
Sentimentalists'
versus 'The
Sufferers'.

disease agents and other miseries, from herpes and kidney tumours
to eye infections and endocarditis.

For many people, medical research to improve the human
condition is acceptable, but there has been a move away from
working with identifiable whole animals. 'Rabbit complement'
and 'baby rabbit complement' are produced from the blood of
living rabbits, but packaged and sold somewhat in the way that
hamburger is distanced from living cow. A quick review of the
literature of biological research reveals that the rabbit is a verit-
able grocery store of useful experimental bits from 'smooth
muscle cells from the rabbit colon' to 'rabbit skin organ culture',
'Alcian blue-treated rabbit gallbladders', 'rabbit corneal cells', and
'rabbit fetal and adult lung'. At some point all these pieces made
up a living rabbit. Very special living rabbits are also available
for experimental research from specialized laboratories, like
Charles River in the United States, which breeds a strain of New
Zealand white first obtained in 1991 from a Japanese lab, and
priced considerably beyond the cost of the average bunny. Charles
River has 'multiple locations around the world' and operates like
the meat industry, 'in a rational, cost-effective, and timely manner'

171

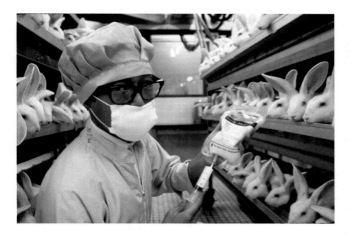

Rabbits used for research on artificial blood, Japan, 1980.

to supply their rabbit products.[29] The industry does have a code of conduct, and rabbits are now euthanized in a 'humane' way, but as one Japanese researcher suggests, 'The euthanasia should be accomplished in a shade of obscurity, considering emotions of other people.'[30] The emotions of the rabbit are not mentioned.

At INRA, the Institute that created the Orylag for the fur industry, the researchers have bred very special rabbits indeed. INRA's work came to international attention in 2000, when Eduardo Kac, an American artist, selected one of the lab's genetically modified rabbits for a bio-art project. He named her Alba. Alba was one of a number of transgenic rabbits 'made' by INRA whose DNA included Green Fluorescent Protein from a jellyfish. Under certain light Alba's pink eyes did indeed glow green, and her skin had a subtle luminescence, though she appears vividly fluorescent on Kac's website. Despite Kac's attempts to 'liberate' her, Alba lived a short, glowing life at the lab, but the GFP bunny lives on in the artist's sketches, photographs and installations, including 'Rabbit in Rio' (Alba's image appears on public clocks), in 'La

'Rabbit test' for nerve gas at the U.S. Army chemical weapons facility Rocky Mountain Arsenal, Colorado, 1970.

Lapin unique', viewed by 1.5 million in Nantes in 2003, in the street sign 'Boulevard Alba,' and in Kac's continuing obsession with drawing rabbits.[31] In 2002, INRA cloned a rabbit, evidently dissatisfied with the natural rate of reproduction.

RABBITS TO SELL

Rabbits are not only sold for meat, fur and body parts, but they are also a global brand. Beyond the products associated with babies and children, from clothes to cutlery, bunnies sell cars, batteries, cereal, teapots, watering cans, chopsticks, dried beans, Bunny-luv carrots, Australian ale (White Rabbit), American beer (Fluffy White Rabbits) and home-brew (Peter Cotton Ale), French Rabbit wine and Rabbit corkscrews, Blue Bunny ice cream, White Rabbit sweets and Brer Rabbit molasses. Rabbit brands and logos capitalize on the rabbit's distinctive shape, so that the outline of a rabbit head, a seated bunny, or a leaping and running rabbit, are easily rendered as strong and identifiable graphics. The Volkswagen Rabbit's logo shows a rabbit running at full gallop, while the Michigan Bean Company chose a leaping rabbit, perhaps symbolic of 'Hopping John', a famous dish of the American South made with black-eyed peas.

Like Peter Rabbit, the representatives of some rabbit brands wear bow ties and neat jackets, while the 'Blue Bunny' is dressed as a 1930s soda jerk. The Energizer Bunny is perhaps the most famous of bunny-branded products. Pink, plush, with sunglasses

The famous 'HERE IT IS' billboard for the Jack Rabbit Trading Post souvenir and crafts shop on Route 66 at Joseph City, Arizona.

and attitude, he beats his drum non-stop, the trickster rabbit with cocky grin, waking up the neighbours and keeping going all night long. He is CBO (Chief Bunny Officer) of Energizer Corporation, has his own Facebook page and, as the Hot Hare Balloon, stands 4 metres (15 feet) taller than the Statue of Liberty. And who can resist Energizer bunny slippers, or a t-shirt, to display 'your Energizer Bunny spirit?'[32]

Bunnies are also easily transformed into objects that amuse, confuse and often charm us. The Bunny Museum in Pasadena, California, displays an 'Elvis Parsley' china figurine created by the American manufacturer Fitz and Floyd, which sells a line of rabbit 'collectibles' from Hoppy Days Teapot to Debutante Bunnies figurines.[33] There is sly humour in many of these creations, as the rabbit morphs so easily into the human. Once on his or her hind legs, unlike the dog or cat forced to walk on two feet, the rabbit seems a natural biped, the proportions translatable to the human form, and the 'baby face' with its impossible ears adding a piquant charm.

THE COMFORT OF RABBIT

It is in the end the rabbit's charm that sells the creatures to us. In Japan, 2012, which is not the Year of the Rabbit, became the year of the rabbit cafe. Customers 'hop' to these pet cafes for a spot of 'cuteness and cuddles'. In Nagoya the manager of the 'Rabbit Sun Cafe' (Usagi Cafe Ohisama) attributed some of this new-found popularity to the natural and man-made disasters that afflicted the Japanese in 2011: 'There are wounds that human beings can't treat but the rabbit can. Rabbits can comfort people without words.'[34] The sixteenth-century Spanish poet St John of the Cross also understood the comfort of rabbit:

A Rabbit Noticed My Condition

I was sad one day and went for a walk;
I sat in a field.

A rabbit noticed my condition and
came near.

It often does not take more than that to help at times –

to just be close to creatures who
are so full of knowing,
so full of love
that they don't
– chat,

they just gaze with
their
marvelous understanding.[35]

Rabbits with
special needs:
Woolly the Rabbit
and his wheels,
Surrey, 2005.

It was that mute comfort that made me an aficionado of the house rabbit. In 1980 after a series of troubling losses, it was our rabbit, Thumps, who helped heal my wounds, lying warm beside me, licking my hand with her small, rough tongue. We acquired the rabbit in the way of so many casual transactions, a 'gift' from a friend on a farm. So small, so cute, why not? Thumps grew to be a very large rabbit, spending her nights in a hutch in the kitchen and her days exploring, lippity-lippity, around the house. We learned about rabbit-proofing electrical cords, and about advising guests not to leave tempting jackets slung over chairs; we made special rabbit biscuits, and tried to convince Thumps to walk with a harness (we failed). We delighted in her antics and she was a topic of dinner conversation for our often astonished friends. She died silently, without complaint, and we buried her in the garden, and immediately sought out another rabbit.

By 1985 we were more than ready for Marinell Harriman's *House Rabbit Handbook,* which affirmed our realization that 'rabbits have been mislabeled, misunderstood and underrated as pets'.[36] The rabbit is the third animal to which we have given the freedom of our homes. Unlike the dog, however, the rabbit is domesticated in name only. Even the most sluggardly of hutch rabbits keeps a wild gleam in her eye and a memory of dancing in the moonlight. Establishing the relationship between rabbit and companion human is the work of long, silent communion, of a softness and a respect for the mute, the vulnerable and the distant. The rabbit is so other, so contained in a world not human, that learning to speak rabbit requires us to settle deeply into that place where we are ourselves but a species among species, sharing an ancient inheritance and a longing for Eden.

Anchorage, Alaska. Friday 16 September 2011. 10:58 P.M. EDT

(Reuters) A pet rabbit is being credited for saving its owners from a house fire in southeastern Alaska before it died of smoke inhalation, fire officials said on Friday.

The rabbit woke up the homeowner early on Tuesday morning by scratching on her chest, the Ketchikan Fire Department said in a statement.

. . .

While there were no injuries to the mother or daughter, the rabbit was not so lucky. The animal succumbed to smoke inhalation and did not survive, the fire department said.[37]

Jean-François
Millet, *Rabbit
Warren, Dawn*,
1867.

A Few Rabbit Poems

Essay on Myxomatosis

Fence hugging I steer the car
down past the shed, the electric
rip of comb or cutter on abrasive
paper suppressing the roll of the frenetic
engine. The track heaves and shuffles,
rises and falls, rolls and dips
as slowly I approach the fading creek.
A shadow swallows the bonnet, I ease
to a stop and slip into neutral,
engaging the handbrake. A great
wedge-tailed eagle settles
in the stubble and starts to
lunge with prehistoric movements
towards a point between car and creek,
one eye on the car, the other on a rabbit
that has appeared on the track.
I open the door and lift myself out
of the seat. The eagle hesitates,
its beak agape like a gargoyle longing
for rain after drought. The rabbit
weaves tightening circles, the sun

blends with haze and shimmer,
a triangle of hunter and hunted,
the curious, afraid, and determined.
The rabbit stops. I draw closer.
The eagle braces its wings like a sail
ripped out of calm waters by storm winds,
spearing sight between us. The rabbit
turns towards me. Its eyes tumorous,
swollen. It targets me blindly, turns
towards the eagle which drops its wings
and lifts softly, tacking into the breeze,
its tension dispersed over the bronze
field, evaporating, eroding the song
of the grinder.
　　The rabbit moves slowly
into the field, reading the braille
of pasture, its head rising and falling
with the tide of stubble.

John Kinsella (1963–)[1]

The White Rabbit

He is white as Helvellyn when winter is well in;
His whiskers are mobile and tender.
If it weren't for the greed that compels him to feed
Without ceasing, his form would be slender.

With elegant hops he crushes or crops
All the flowers that bloom in the garden;
Yet such is the grace that suffuses his face,
He wins, without asking, our pardon.

The Sun, who rides heaven from Dover to Devon
Inspecting furred folks and their habits,
Breaks out into poesy: 'What summer snow is he
Made of, this pearl among rabbits?'

And at night on the lawn as he waits for the dawn,
Rapt in dreams of a rabbit's perfection,
The moon in her stride sweeps the cloudlets aside
To rejoice in his silver reflection.

Emile Victor Rieu (1887–1972)[2]

The Rabbit has an evil mind
Although he looks so good and kind.
His life is a complete disgrace,
Although he has so soft a face.
I hardly like to let you know
How far his wickedness will go.
Enough, if this poor rhyme declares
His fearful cruelty to hares.
He does his very best to keep
These gentle animals from sleep,
By joining in with noisy throngs
Of rabbits singing ribald songs.
To wake their fears and make them bound,
He stimulates the Basset-hound.
And if he meets them after dark,
He imitates the greyhound's bark.

Lord Alfred Douglas (1870–1945)[3]

Timeline of the Rabbit

55 MYA	5–3 MYA	77–9 AD	1176

First appearance in Asia of recognizable lagomorphs

Nuralagus rex, an extinct giant rabbit, roams the island of Minorca

Pliny the Elder describes a rabbit plague on Minorca and Majorca

The first European rabbits arrive in Britain, on the Scilly Islands

1865	1881	1901–7	1902

Alice follows the White Rabbit down the rabbit hole in Lewis Carroll's *Alice's Adventures in Wonderland*

Joel Chandler Harris publishes *Uncle Remus, His Songs and His Sayings*, introducing Brer Rabbit to a wider audience

Western Australia constructs the wire mesh equivalent of the Great Wall of China, No. 1 Rabbit Proof Fence, 1,770 km long

Beatrix Potter's *The Tale of Peter Rabbit* is a publishing sensation

1953	1960	1972	1984

Myxomatosis travels across the Channel to Britain on the backs of birds and in farmers' cars

Hugh Hefner presents the first Playboy Bunnies

Richard Adams introduces us to Hazel, Bigwig and Fiver in *Watership Down*

Rabbit Hemorrhagic Disease (RHD) is identified in China

1555	1777	1859	1876	1879
The naturalist Conrad Gesner wonders at the abundance of rabbits in England	Captain James Cook releases European rabbits on Motuara Island off New Zealand	Thomas Austin releases thirteen European rabbits on his estate at Geelong, Australia, to provide 'sport'	New Zealand passes its first Rabbit Nuisance Act	Australia passes its first Rabbit Destruction Act

1925	1942	1947	1950	1952
Rabbit lovers in the United States found the American Rabbit Breeders Association (ARBA)	Margaret Wise Brown creates *The Runaway Bunny*	New Zealand establishes the Rabbit Destruction Council	The myxomatosis virus is introduced into the Australian rabbit population	Dr Delille, hero to farmers, villain to rabbit raisers, releases myxomatosis on his estate at Maillebois in France

1985	1988	1991	FEB 2011 – JAN 2012
Marinell Harriman publishes *The House Rabbit Handbook: How to Live with an Urban Rabbit*	The House Rabbit Society is founded in California	The Foundation for Rabbit-Free Australia replaces the Easter Bunny with the Easter Bilby, a large-eared native marsupial	Chinese Zodiac Year of the Rabbit

References

1 A NATURAL HISTORY

1 Albert E. Wood, 'What, if Anything, is a Rabbit?', *Evolution*, 11 (December 1957), pp. 417–25.

2 James W. Gidley, 'The Lagomorphs, an Independent Order', *Science*, new ser., XXXVI/922 (30 August 1912), pp. 285–6, p. 285. On the relation to antelope and deer, Gidley was referencing an article of 1884 by the palaeontologist Edward Drinker Cope.

3 Alison K. Surridge, Robert J. Timmins, Godfrey M. Hewitt and Diana J. Bell, 'Striped Rabbits in Southeast Asia', *Nature*, 400 (19 August 1999), p. 726.

4 Pedro Durant and Manuel A. Guevara, 'A New Rabbit Species (*Sylvilagus*, Mammalia: Leporidae) from the Lowlands of Venezuela', *Revista de Biología Tropical*, XLI/1 (March 2001).

5 Wood, 'What, if Anything, is a Rabbit?', p. 417.

6 Mark Elbroch and Kurt Rinehart, *Behavior of North American Mammals*, Peterson Reference Guide (New York, 2011), p. 39.

7 Ivan R. Tomkins, 'The Marsh Rabbit: An Incomplete Life History', *Journal of Mammalogy*, XVI/3 (August 1935), pp. 201–5, p. 203.

8 Charles E. Lowe, 'Ecology of the Swamp Rabbit in Georgia', *Journal of Mammalogy*, XXXIX/1 (February 1958), pp. 116–27, p. 120.

9 Ronald M. Lockley, *The Private Life of the Rabbit* (London, 1976), p. 26.

10 Richard Adams, *Watership Down* (New York, 1972), p. 26.

11 Elbroch and Rinehart, *Behavior of North American Mammals*,
   p. 42.
12 A. F. Carr, Jr, 'Notes on Escape Behavior in the Florida Marsh
   Rabbit', *Journal of Mammalogy*, xx/3 (August 1939), pp. 322–5,
   p. 323.
13 'Anti-hunting: Hunting – "The Murderous Business"', IDA
   International, www.idausa.com, accessed 20 February 2012.
14 '*Bunolagus monticularis*', at The IUCN List of Threatened Species,
   www.iucnredlist.org, accessed 18 February 2012.
15 In 2009 the Polish film *Królik po berlinsku* (*Rabbit à la Berlin*),
   the story of the rabbits who live in the no-man's-land between
   the walls, was nominated for an Oscar.
16 Susan E. Davis and Margo DeMello, *Stories Rabbits Tell: A Natural
   and Cultural History of a Misunderstood Creature* (New York, 2003),
   pp. 23–4.
17 M. E. Coates, Margaret E. Gregory and S. Y. Thompson, 'The
   Composition of Rabbit's Milk', *British Journal of Nutrition*,
   18 (1964), pp. 583–6, p. 584.
18 Ernest Thompson Seton, *Wild Animals I Have Known* (Toronto,
   2006), pp. xi–xiii.
19 Ibid., p. 57.
20 John James Audubon and J. Bachman, *The Imperial Collection
   of Audubon Animals: The Quadrupeds of North America* (New York,
   1967), p. 28.

2 THE NATURAL AND UNNATURAL HISTORY OF THE EUROPEAN RABBIT

1 Win Kirkpatrick, Amanda Page and Marion Massam, 'European
  Rabbit (*Oryctolagus cuniculus*) Risk Assessment for Australia',
  Department of Agriculture and Food, Western Australia (August,
  2008), p. 10.
2 It has been suggested that the name 'Hispania' may derive from
  the Punic (the language of Carthage) for 'island of hyrax', and
  though the hyrax is a different creature, it superficially resembles
  the rabbit.

3 John C. E. Flux, 'World Distribution', in H. V. Thompson and C. M. King, *The European Rabbit: The History and Biology of a Successful Colonizer* (Oxford, 1994) pp. 8–21, p. 14.

4 '*Oryctolagus cuniculus*', at The IUCN List of Threatened Species, www.iucnredlist.org, accessed 3 March 2012.

5 Flux, 'World Distribution', p. 17.

6 Though these were not the first lagomorphs on the island. Researchers recently discovered the fossil of a giant prehistoric rabbit, *Nuralagus rex*, the 'Rabbit King'. J. Quintana, M. Köhler and S. Moyà-Solà, '*Nuralagus rex*, gen.et.sp. nov., an Endemic Insular Giant Rabbit from the Neogene of Minorca (Balearic Islands, Spain)', *Journal of Vertebrate Paleontology*, XXXI/2 (2011), www.vertpaleo.org.

7 Polybius, *Histories*, trans. Evelyn S. Shuckburgh (New York, 1889, reprinted Bloomington, IN, 1962), Book 12, chapter 3. These may, however, have been the now extinct Sardinian pika (*Prolagus sardus*), according to recent studies by J. D. Vigne, 'Zooarchaeology and the Biogeographical History of the Mammals of Corsica and Sardinia since the Last Ice Age', *Mammalogy Review*, XXII/2 (1992), pp. 87–96.

8 Strabo, *Geography* (London, 1903), Book 3, chapter 2, section 6.

9 Juliet Clutton-Brock, *A Natural History of Domesticated Mammals* (Cambridge, 1987), p. 144.

10 Strabo, *Geography*, Book 3, chapter 2, section 6.

11 Pliny the Elder, *The Natural History*, ed. John Bostock and Henry Thomas Riley, 2nd edn (London, 1855), Book 8: 'The Nature of the Terrestrial Animals', chapter 43, section 29: 'Nations That Have Been Exterminated by Animals'.

12 Ibid., chapter 81, section 55: 'The Different Species of Hares'.

13 Apicius, *The Roman Cookery Book*, trans. Barbara Flower and Elisabeth Rosenbaum (London, 1961), pp. 66–7; Pliny the Elder, *The Natural History*, Book 8, chapter 81, section 55.

14 John Sheail, *Rabbits and Their History* (Newton Abbot, 1972), pp. 36–7.

15 C. Gesner, *Historiae animalium*, trans. E. Topsell (London, 1607), p. 110, quoted in Elspeth Veale, 'The Rabbit in England', *The Agricultural History Review*, v/2 (1957), pp. 85–90, p. 90.

16 Sheail, *Rabbits and Their History*, p. 44.

17 Ibid., p. 48

18 Ibid., p. 59

19 Olivier de Serres, *Le Théâtre d'agriculture et mesnage des champs*, 3rd edn (Paris, 1605), p. 413.

20 Sheail, *Rabbits and Their History*, pp. 17, 62.

21 These might have been the South American tapeti, or perhaps European rabbits imported from Holland to stock the garden. Maria Angélica da Silva and Melissa Mota Alcides, 'Collecting and Framing the Wilderness: The Gardens of Johan Maurits (1604–79) in North-East Brazil', *Garden History*, xxx/2, 'Dutch Influences' (Winter 2002), pp. 153–76, p. 167.

22 Thomas Pennant, *British Zoology* (London, 1776), vol. i, p. 105

23 Sheail, *Rabbits and Their History*, p. 111

24 Lawrence H. Officer and Samuel H. Williamson, 'Purchasing Power of British Pounds from 1245 to Present' (2013), www. measuringworth.com/ppoweruk.

25 Jean M. Ingersoll, 'The Australian Rabbit', *American Scientist*, lii/2 (June 1964), pp. 265–73, p. 265. Not all these introductions were successful, and on many islands in the Caribbean, Indian Ocean and Pacific, the European rabbit failed to thrive, or was eliminated. See Kirkpatrick et al., 'European Rabbit (*Oryctolagus cuniculus*) Risk Assessment', pp. 6–9.

26 D. G. Stead, *The Rabbit in Australia*, quoted in Flux, 'World Distribution', p. 12.

27 Thompson and King, *The European Rabbit*, p. xiii.

28 'PestSmart Factsheet: Rabbit Legislation in Australia', www.feral.org.uk, accessed 17 March 2012.

29 Ingersoll, 'The Australian Rabbit', p. 268. But only theoretical, since even in Australia, only 1 to 10 per cent of young survive to adulthood.

30 Mark Twain, *Following the Equator: A Journey around the World* (Hartford, CT, 1897), pp. 101–2.

31 As recently as 1969 piles of dead rabbits had to be removed using
    a bulldozer from the South Australian side of the New South
    Wales–South Australian border fence. It is possible these mass-
    directional movements are triggered by rain many kilometres
    away. I. Parer, 'Dispersal of the Wild Rabbit, *Oryctolagus cuniculus*,
    at Urana in New South Wales', *Australian Wildlife Research*, 9
    (1982), pp. 427–41.

32 'Rabbit Problems in Australia', www.animalcontrol.com.au,
    accessed 17 March 2012.

33 'Weird, True and Freaky: Outback Rabbit Invasion', Animal
    Planet, www.animal.discovery.com, accessed 3 March 2012.

34 'Earthweek: Australian Rabbit Plague Emerging' (17 February
    2012), www.earthweek.com.

35 Robert Peden, 'Rabbits: The Spread of Rabbits in New Zealand',
    Te Ara: The Encyclopedia of New Zealand (updated 1 March 2009),
    www.TeAra.govt.nz.

36 Select Committtee, *Reference: Appendix to the Journals of
    the House of Representatives (New Zealand)* (1876), pp. 1–5,
    p. 4, in Peden, 'Rabbits: Rabbits' Impact on Farming', *Te Ara:
    The Encyclopedia of New Zealand* (updated 1 March 2009),
    www.TeAra.govt.nz.

37 Ibid.

38 C. K. Williams, I. Parer, B. J. Coman, J. Burley and M. L. Braysher,
    Managing Vertebrate Pests: Rabbits, Bureau of Resource Sciences/
    csiro Division of Wildlife and Ecology, Australian Government
    Publishing Service (Canberra, 1995), p. 104.

39 The Intercolonial Rabbit Commission in Australia offered
    a £25,000 reward for a practical method of control, and
    determination 'as to whether the introduction of disease amongst
    rabbits by inoculation or otherwise, or the propagation of
    diseases natural to rabbits, for the purpose of destroying or
    promoting their destruction, would be accompanied by danger
    to human or animal life'. Report in the *Sydney Morning Herald*
    (17 April 1888), www.trove.nla.gov.au.

40 Sheail, *Rabbits and Their History*, p. 179.

41 See Stephen Dando-Collins, *Pasteur's Gambit: Louis Pasteur, the Australasian Rabbit Plague, and a Ten Million Dollar Prize* (North Sydney, 2008).

42 Ronald M. Lockley, *The Private Life of the Rabbit* (London, 1976), p. 130.

43 John Kinsella, 'Essay on Myxomatosis', in *The Silo: A Pastoral Symphony* (1995), www.poetrylibrary.edu.au.

44 Thompson and King, *The European Rabbit*, p. xiii.

45 Brian Cooke, 'Making the Most of Rabbit Haemorrhagic Disease' (May 2003), www.agric.wa.gov.au/objtwr/imported_assets/ content/pw/vp/rab/rhd_booklet_may03.pdf, accessed 1 April 2012.

46 Williams et al., *Managing Vertebrate Pests: Rabbits*, p. 32.

47 Foundation for Rabbit-Free Australia Inc., 'Easter Bilby Campaign: The Beginning of the Easter Bilby', www.rabbitfreeaustralia. org.au, accessed 7 April 2012.

3 THE 'USEFUL' RABBIT

1 Robert Mark and Evelyn Billo, 'Pictographs at Hunters Shelter: Possible Extension of the Red Linear Style into the Guadalupe Mountains of Southern New Mexico', *Plains Anthropologist*, LIV/211 (2009), pp. 201–10.

2 As recounted in Edward S. Curtis, *The North American Indian*, vol. XII: *The Hopi* (Norwood, MA, 1922), p. 45.

3 'J.M.S.', 'A Pueblo Rabbit-Hunt', *The Journal of American Folklore*, VIII/31 (October–December 1895), pp. 324–7.

4 Elspeth Veale, 'The Rabbit in England', *The Agricultural History Review*, V (1957), pp. 85–90, p. 89.

5 John Sheail, *Rabbits and Their History* (Newton Abbot, 1972) p. 78.

6 *Le Ménagier de Paris* (a medieval manuscript dated to around 1393), edited by Jérome Pichon in 1846 for La Société des Bibliophiles Français, www.pbm.com/~lindahl/menagier, accessed 9 April 2012.

7 Ken Albala, *Eating Right in the Renaissance* (Berkeley, CA, 2002), pp. 80, 168. While eating rabbits might make people timid, eating nothing but rabbit can make them sick. 'Rabbit starvation' is a form of malnutrition caused by eating nothing but lean meat, which the human body cannot convert into adequate energy. When only rabbit was available, the Athapascan peoples of northwest Canada could starve in the midst of plenty.

8 Young rabbits are best in March and suitable food for 'old melancholick dry, and weak stomachs', according to Thomas Muffet in *Health's Improvement; or, Rules Comprising and Discovering the Nature, Method, and Manner of Preparing All Sorts of Food Used in This Nation* (London, 1655), pp. 76–7, available at Library of Congress Online Catalog, http://catalog.loc.gov, accessed 9 April 2012.

9 Charles Estienne and Jean Liébault, *L'Agriculture et maison rustique* (Rouen, 1658), p. 606.

10 Sheail, *Rabbits and Their History*, p. 27.

11 William Cobbett, *Cottage Economy* (New York, 1833), pp. 111–13.

12 *The Cultivator*, new ser., II (Albany, NY, 1845), p. 174, www.books.google.ca, accessed 9 April 2012.

13 Gervase Markham, *A Way to Get Wealth* (London, 1668), p. 109.

14 David Yoder, Jon Blood and Mason Reid, 'How Warm Were They? Thermal Properties of Rabbit Skin Robes and Blankets', *Journal of California and Great Basin Anthropology*, XXV/1 (2005), pp. 55–68.

15 Olivia Remie Constable, *Trade and Traders in Muslim Spain: The Commercial Realignment of the Iberian Peninsula, 900–1500*, Cambridge Studies in Medieval Life and Thought, 4th ser., 24 (Cambridge, 1996), p. 219.

16 Mark Bailey, 'The Rabbit and the Medieval East Anglian Economy', *Agriculture History Review*, XXXVI/1 (1988), pp. 1–20, p. 12.

17 As, for example, in the edition of 1551 printed in Zurich: Turning the Pages Online, National Library of Medicine, http://archive.nlm.nih.gov/proj/ttp, accessed 12 April 2012.

18 Noted in Charles Darwin, *The Variation of Plants and Animals under Domestication* [1868] (London, 1905), p. 127.

19 John Mortimer, *The Whole Art of Husbandry; or, The Way of Managing and Improving of Land* (London, 1708), p. 189.

20 R. J. Lloyd Price, *Rabbits for Profit and Rabbits for Powder: A Treatise on the New Industry of Hutch Farming in the Open, and upon Warrens Specially Intended for Sporting Purposes* (London, 1884), p. vii.

21 Caleb N. Bement, *The Rabbit Fancier* (New York, 1859), p. 13. Bement copied large portions of his work from an earlier treatise by Eugene Delamer, *Pigeons and Rabbits in their Wild, Domestic and Captive States* (London, 1854).

22 A favourite dish of Alexandre Dumas *père*, from his *Grand Dictionnaire de Cuisine* (1873), translated by Alan and Jane Davidson as *Dumas on Food* (Oxford, 1987), p. 239. Dumas also cautioned against rabbit tampering. Clapper conies (*lapin de choux*) were singed or dyed to mimic the reddish fur of the feet and tail of the more desirable wild rabbit (*lapin de garenne*).

23 George F. Morant, *Rabbits as Food Supply: How to Fold Them on Our Poor Pastures* (London, 1883), p. 4.

24 Charles Elmé Francatelli, *A Plain Cookery Book for the Working Classes* (Whitstable, 1993), p. 38.

25 Sheail, *Rabbits and Their History*, p. 80.

26 Lloyd Price, *Rabbits for Profit*, pp. 2–3.

27 Sheail, *Rabbits and Their History*, p. 79.

28 Ibid., p. 81.

29 Charles Varlo, *A New System of Husbandry* (Philadelphia, 1785), vol. II, p. 81.

30 Bement, *The Rabbit Fancier*, p. 17.

31 François Lebas, 'Origine du lapin et domestication', www.cuniculture.info, accessed 9 April 2012.

32 *Fur Trade Review*, XIX (1891), p. 165.

33 Quoted in Susan E. Davis and Margo DeMello, *Stories Rabbits Tell: A Natural and Cultural History of a Misunderstood Creature* (New York, 2003), p. 270.

34 Mortimer, *The Whole Art of Husbandry*, p. 189. Angora is thought to be a corruption of Ankhara, hence, the 'Turky' rabbit. Whether or not the breed originated in Turkey is unclear, since

in earlier times any exotic animal or plant might be said to have come from the mysterious East, and so the archetypal North American bird becomes the turkey and Indian corn is transformed into Turkey wheat.

35 'Fuzzy Fad Distresses Lint-covered Escorts', *Life* (19 December 1938), p. 40.

36 'Angora: Pictorial Records of an ss Experiment', *The Wisconsin Magazine of History*, L/4, Unpublished Documents on Nazi Germany from the Mass Communications History Center (Summer 1967), pp. 392–413, p. 396.

37 Darwin, *The Variation of Plants and Animals*, pp. 130–32.

38 Luther Tucker, 'Breeding and Management of the Rabbit', *The Cultivator* (May 1851), pp. 176–8.

39 Bement, *The Rabbit Fancier*, p. 73.

40 'Au 20e siècle: Passage de l'élevage de tradition à l'élevage rationnel', www.cuniculture.info, accessed 2 June 2012.

41 Sheail, *Rabbits and Their History*, p. 113.

42 Lloyd Price, *Rabbits for Profit*, p. 32.

4 RABBIT IN MIND

1 In China and Japan, the calendar rabbit was originally a hare, China having no native rabbits and Japan only the reclusive Amami rabbit. European rabbits came to China along the silk routes, and they were introduced to the island kingdom in the sixteenth century, probably by the Portuguese or perhaps later by the Dutch. In iconography and popular culture, the softer contours and appealing manner of the rabbit have now largely replaced the hare's rangier form and more distant character.

2 Liu Lan, 'Year of the Rabbit', *Beijing Review* (3 February 2011), www.bjreview.com.

3 Li Bai, 'The Old Dust', www.poemhunter.com, accessed 7 May 2012.

4 Schuyler Cammann, 'Ming Festival Symbols', *Archives of the Chinese Art Society of America*, VII (1953), pp. 66–70, p. 68.

5   Rudolf Wittkower, 'Eagle and Serpent: A Study in the Migration
    of Symbols', *Journal of the Warburg Institute*, II/4 (April 1939),
    pp. 293–325, p. 305.

6   John M. McBryde, Jr, 'Brer Rabbit in the Folk-Tales of the Negro
    and Other Races', *The Sewanee Review*, XIX/2 (April 1911),
    pp. 185–206, p. 192.

7   The African American trickster Brer Rabbit also uses hot peppers
    that he rubs on the inside of a witch's skin to prevent her from
    resuming her human form in the light of day, and leading to her
    killing by the animals. See the tale of Brer Rabbit and Ol' Mammy
    Witch-Wise in Emma M. Backus, 'Tales of the Rabbit from
    Georgia Negroes', *The Journal of American Folklore*, XII/45
    (April–June 1899), pp. 108–15, 110.

8   Elizabeth Coatsworth, 'Song of the Rabbits Outside the Tavern',
    The Saturday Review (15 September 1934), p. 113.

9   See this family of stories in William H. Mechling, 'Stories
    from Tuxtepec, Oaxaca', *The Journal of American Folklore*,
    XXV/97 (July–September 1912), pp. 199–203, p. 202; J. Kunst,
    'Some Animal Fables of the Chuh Indians', *The Journal of
    American Folklore*, XXVII/110 (October–December 1915),
    pp. 353–7, p. 356.

10 Joel Chandler Harris, *Uncle Remus, His Songs and His Sayings:
    The Folklore of the Old Plantation* (New York, 1881), p. 9.

11 Cameron C. Nickels, 'An Early Version of the "Tar Baby" Story',
    The Journal of American Folklore, XCIV/373 (July–September 1981),
    pp. 364–9, p. 363.

12 A folklorist in the 1930s counted 158 versions of this tale world-
    wide, with 29 among Native Americans, where the tar is sometimes
    pine gum. Noted in Sandra K. Baringer, 'Brer Rabbit and His
    Cherokee Cousin: Moving Beyond the Appropriation Paradigm',
    in *When Brer Rabbit Meets Coyote: African-Native American Literature*,
    ed. Jonathan Brennan (Champaign, IL, 2003), pp. 114–38, p. 116.

13 Gerard Fowke, 'Brer Rabbit and Brer Fox: How Brer Rabbit was
    Allowed to Choose His Death', *The Journal of American Folklore*,
    I/2 (July–September 1888), pp. 148–9.

14 Linda Lear, *Beatrix Potter: A Life in Nature* (New York, 2007), p. 131.
15 Ibid., p. 73.
16 Beatrix Potter, quoted ibid., p. 183.
17 'News Releases: Peter Rabbit Publishing Set to Launch in China!', www.prnewswire.co.uk, accessed 5 May 2012.
18 The publisher has also commissioned the British actress Emma Thompson to write *The Further Tale of Peter Rabbit*. See 'Contemporary Retelling of *The Tale of Peter Rabbit* in this year's Booktime Packs to Celebrate 110 Years of Beatrix Potter's Much-Loved Character', press release (3 May 2012), www.pearson.com.
19 'You hear, sah, how Brer Rabbit's left foot fetch you luck when you tote it constant in your pocket. It most surely do that, sah, 'cause that Ole Brer Rabbit be just born to luck.' Backus, 'Tales of the Rabbit from Georgia Negroes', p. 111.
20 A. R. Wright and E. Lovett, 'Specimens of Modern Mascots and Ancient Amulets of the British Isles', *Folklore*, ix/3 (September 1908), pp. 288–303, p. 296.
21 Frank Lebby Stanton was the poet laureate of Georgia in the 1920s. 'The Graveyard Rabbit', in Edmund Clarence Stedman, ed., *An American Anthology, 1787–1900* (Boston, ma, 1900; Bartleby.com, 2001), accessed 3 May 2012. The Graveyard Rabbits is the name of an organization dedicated to the preservation and maintenance of historic cemeteries.
22 Bill Ellis, 'Why Is a Lucky Rabbit's Foot Lucky? Body Parts as Fetishes', *Journal of Folklore Research*, xxxix/1 (January–April 2002), pp. 51–84, p. 69.
23 Ibid., p. 61
24 Michael Houseman, 'Le Tabou du lapin chez les marins: Une spéculation structurale', *Ethnologie Française*, new ser., xx/2, 'Figures animales' (April–June 1990), pp. 125–42, p. 128.
25 Wright and Lovett, 'Specimens of Modern Mascots', pp. 295–6.
26 Iona and Peter Opie, *The Lore and Language of Schoolchildren* (Oxford, 1987), p. 226.
27 W.H.D. Rouse, 'Tokens of Death', *Folklore*, iv/2 (June 1893), p. 258.

28 Jacqueline Simpson and Stephen Roud, 'Rabbit', in *Oxford Dictionary of English Folklore* (Oxford), n.p.
29 M. P. Watkins, 'Witch-Rabbits in Devonshire', *Folklore*, LX/1 (March 1957), p. 296.
30 Ellis, 'Why Is a Lucky Rabbit's Foot Lucky?', p. 68.
31 Richard Adams, *Watership Down* (New York, 1972), p. 241.
32 Potter wrote his obituary: 'In affectionate remembrance of poor old Peter Rabbit, who died on the 26th of January 1901 at the end of his 9th year . . . whatever the limitations of his intellect or outward shortcomings of his fur, and his ears and toes, his disposition was uniformly amiable and his temper unfailingly sweet. An affectionate companion and a quiet friend.' Quoted in 'Beatrix Potter: *The Tale of Peter Rabbit*', www.vam.ac.uk, accessed 5 May 2012.
33 DuBose Heyward, *The Country Bunny and the Little Gold Shoes* (Boston, 1967), n.p.
34 Ibid.

5 RABBITS AND US

1 Ronald Lockley, *The Private Life of the Rabbit* (London, 1976), p. 164.
2 Ibid., p. 13.
3 'But they are all pretty objects, and since we have kept our rabbits in the open air, on the green grass, a visit to them has become a pleasure.' George F. Morant, *Rabbits as Food Supply: How to Fold Them on Our Poor Pastures* (London, 1883), p. 21.
4 Caleb N. Bement, *The Rabbit Fancier* (New York, 1859), p. 12.
5 Ibid., p. 46.
6 R. O. Edwards, *Rabbits for Exhibition, Pleasure, and Market, Being a Complete Guide for the Amateur and Professional Rabbit Keeper* (London, 1884), p. 10.
7 Bement, *The Rabbit Fancier*, p. 17.
8 Morant, *Rabbits as Food Supply*, pp. 39, 4.
9 Ivy L. Wallace, *Pookie* (London, 1946), n.p.

10 M. Daphne Kutzer, writing about Potter, suggests that 'Rabbits, in fact, may be seen as her alter-ego during the first phase of her career.' Kutzer, *Beatrix Potter: Writing in Code* (New York, 2003), p. 38.

11 Margaret Wise Brown, *The Runaway Bunny* (New York, 1942), n.p.

12 Ernest Thompson Seton, *Wild Animals I Have Known* (Toronto, 2006), p. xiii.

13 Ernest Thompson Seton, *The Wild Animal Play for Children with Alternate Reading for Very Young Children* (New York, 1900), pp. 54–7.

14 Ibid., p. 64.

15 Ervin S. Chapman, *Particeps criminis: The Story of a California Rabbit Drive* (New York, 1910), pp. 68–9.

16 Ibid., pp. 90–91.

17 Ibid., p. 14.

18 Joel Chandler Harris, *Uncle Remus, His Songs and His Sayings: The Folklore of the Old Plantation* (New York, 1881), p. 130.

19 Jacob Ludwig Grimm and Wilhelm Carl Grimm, 'The Rabbit's Bride', *Grimms' Fairy Tales* [1812], www.grimmstories.com, accessed 1 June 2012.

20 Gervase Markham, *A Way to Get Wealth* (London, 1668), pp. 107–8.

21 D. H. Lawrence, *Women in Love* [1920], chapter 18, 'Rabbit', www.gutenberg.org, accessed 6 May 2012.

22 The eighteenth-century French scientist René Antoine Ferchault de Réaumur insisted he had seen coupling between a rabbit and a hen; he was not widely believed in scientific circles. François Lebas, 'Origine du lapin et domestication', www.cuniculture.info, accessed 6 May 2012.

23 'The Curious Case of Mary Toft' (August 2009), http://special.lib.gla.ac.uk.

24 *The Doctors in Labour; or, A new Whim Wham from Guildford* (1726), in Hunterian Aa.7.20, http://special.lib.gla.ac.uk, accessed 12 May 2012.

25 In one contemporaneous poem, 'The Rabbit-Man-Midwife', the author suggests that 'Bunny's Dad must be a Lord, / Whose

Name does end in Burrough'. From *A New Miscellany*, attrib. John Arbuthnot (London, 1730).

26 Michael Houseman, 'Le Tabou du lapin chez les marins: Une spéculation structurale', *Ethnologie Française*, new ser., xx/2e, 'Figures animales' (April–June 1990), pp. 125–42, p. 127.

27 Ibid., p. 128.

28 Claude K. Abraham, 'Myth and Symbol: The Rabbit in Medieval France', *Studies in Philology*, LX/4 (October 1963), pp. 589–97, p. 593.

29 And continues to be used today, though increasingly rarely, when women are referred to as 'dumb bunnies'.

30 Susan E. Davis and Margo DeMello, *Stories Rabbits Tell: A Natural and Cultural History of a Misunderstood Animal* (New York, 2003), pp. 215–16.

31 Simon Carnell, *Hare* (London, 2010), p. 60.

32 Mark Ryder, 'Artist Statement', *Wondertoonel Exhibition Catalogue*, www.wondertoonel.com, accessed 12 May 2012.

33 In China, the rabbit's lack of overt external sexual characteristics make it an apt emblem of the princess-warrior Mulan. When she emerges among the troops dressed as a woman, they express great astonishment: 'The male rabbit hops from the beginning; the female rabbit's eyes are misty . . .'. She replies, 'Both rabbits are running along the ground; how can you tell whether I am male or female?' 'The Ballad of Mulan', Literary: Tsoi Dug, www.tsoidug.org, accessed 9 May 2012.

34 Lockley, *The Private Life of the Rabbit*, p. 55.

35 An interviewer asked Sakai, 'Why a rabbit?' His answer: 'He's fun to draw. I was just sketching one day, and I drew a rabbit with his ears tied up into a samurai topknot, and I loved it. He looked great, he looked unique – it was very simple, but no one had ever done it before. And so I kept him as a rabbit.' R. J. Carter, 'Interview: Stan Sakai: Down the Rabbit Hole with Usagi Yojimbo' (5 April 2001), www.the-trades.com.

1 C. Mougenot and L. Strivay, *Le Pire ami de l'homme: Du lapin de garenne aux guerres biologiques* (Paris, 2011), 'Man's Worst Friend' (1 October 2012), http://reflexions.ulg.ac.be.

2 Susan E. Davis and Margo DeMello, *Stories Rabbits Tell: A Natural and Cultural History of a Misunderstood Creature* (New York, 2003), pp. 233–5.

3 Diane Wells, 'Small Livestock: Meat Rabbits and Overcoming the Easter Bunny Syndrome', *Farming, The Journal of Northeast Agriculture* (June 2012), www.farmingmagazine.com.

4 F. Lebas et al., *The Rabbit: Husbandry, Health and Production* (Rome, 1997; revd edn), Food and Agriculture Organization of the United Nations, www.fao.org, accessed 17 May 2012. More recent data from the European Food Safety Authority in 2003 estimates more than 857 million rabbits were slaughtered for the meat industry, with more than half in China. Coalition to Abolish the Fur Trade, 'The Reality of Commercial Rabbit Farming in Europe, http://faada.org/userfiles/CAFT_Rabbit_Fur_Report.pdf, accessed 18 May 2012.

5 Output is measured in TEC, or Tonnes Equivalent Carcass.

6 'Rabbit Production in Developing Countries', www.world-rabbit-science.com, accessed 17 May 2012.

7 'Sichuan Xuping Rabbit Co. Ltd.', www.chinarabbitking.com, accessed 8 September 2012. See also Casey Neese, 'Leadership Lessons from "The Rabbit King"' (3 August 2011), www.heifer.org.

8 In 2008, China produced 660,000 tonnes of rabbit meat, for both domestic and export consumption. 'The Rabbit Market: What Became of the Easter Bunny?', *The Economist*, www.economist.com, 21 April 2011.

9 In 2010 the 'chilled and frozen rabbit meat business became the main profit contributor' for Kangda Foods. *China Kangda Food Company Interim Report* (2010), p. 5, www.kangdafood.com/img/upfilepic/20109261795448030.pdf, accessed 17 May 2012.

10 'Under metal overhangs, the rabbits were housed in two double-sided rows of wire holding cages. The stocking densities ranged from six to eleven rabbits per cage. Each cage was no wider than 1.5 feet. The vast majority of the cages had a high number of rabbits enclosed. As the stocking density increased, the rabbits had greater difficulty moving around. There was a strong ammonia odor from the rabbits' urine and an accumulation of fecal waste below the cages. The bottoms of the cages were layered with cobwebs and rabbit hair. Rabbits in the cages were observed sneezing. The wiring of the cages was corroded. Some of the cages were poorly rigged – denying rabbits stable, level footing.' 'Meat Rabbits and some Statistics', www.rabbitadvocacy.com, accessed 17 May 2012.

11 Recorded in Davis and DeMello, *Stories Rabbits Tell*, p. 241.

12 Bureau of Animal Welfare, Attwood, Code of Practice for the Intensive Husbandry of Rabbits (October 1991), www.dpi.vic.gov.au.

13 Coalition to Abolish the Fur Trade, 'The Reality of Commercial Rabbit Farming in Europe', www.caft.org.uk, accessed 20 May 2012. Protest against the fur trade resulted in the 2004 decision by Inditext (which includes the retailer Zara) to stop offering rabbit fur to customers, a decision much regretted by the IFTF (www.wearefur.com, accessed 20 May 2012).

14 Robert G. Hodgson, *Raising Fur Rabbits* (Toronto, 1927), p. 14.

15 'An Exceptional Fur, Orylag', www.orylag.com, accessed 21 May 2012.

16 'Leopard Fake Fur', Made-in-China.com, accessed 21 May 2012.

17 Lady Rachel Byng, writing in *The Fur Trade Journal*, quoted in Hodgson, *Raising Fur Rabbits*, p. 59.

18 In 2002 there was estimated to be about 50 million Angoras, producing 10,000 tonnes of rabbit 'fibre'. A. C. Schlink and S. M. Liu, *Angora Rabbits: A Potential New Industry for Australia*, Kingston: Rural Industries Research and Development Corporation (April 2003), p. 6.

19 Noted in Caleb N. Bement, *The Rabbit Fancier* (New York, 1859), pp. 76–7. Darwin also welcomed to his home (or hutch) two living

rabbits from Moscow, with snow-white fur and pink eyes, and spent much time observing the breeding of Himalayans, which he called 'these pretty rabbits'. Charles Darwin, *The Variation of Plants and Animals under Domestication* [1868] (London, 1905), p. 108.

20 The British Rabbit Council, Breed Standards, www.thebrc.org, accessed 22 May 2012.

21 Le Club français des éléveurs de lapins Fauve de Bourgogne, http://fauvedebourgogne.pagesperso-orange.fr, accessed 22 May 2012. The club is recognized by the French Federation of Cuniculture.

22 'The South Australian Rabbit Fanciers Society Incorporated', http://thesarabbitfancierss.tripod.com, accessed 1 June 2012. For rabbits on YouTube, see 'Champis – den vallande kaninen', 2012; and 'The REAL "Energizer Bunny"', 2007, at www.youtube.com, accessed 11 June 2012, and www.youtube.com/watch?v=lwM92P8aT64, accessed 25 June 2013.

23 'About the ARBA . . .', www.arba.net, accessed 1 June 2012.

24 The South Australian Rabbit Fanciers Society Incorporated, http://therabbitfanciers.tripod.com, accessed 1 June 2012.

25 'Rabbit Hopping', www.kaninhop.dk/uk, accessed 1 June 2012.

26 The phrase 'the rabbit died', to communicate pregnancy, entered the English language.

27 'Be Nice to Bunnies', iPhone application. See 'Stephanie Pratt Says, 'Be Nice to Bunnies!', www.peta.org.uk, accessed 1 June 2012.

28 Rabbits are the third most widely used small mammals in British laboratories, after rats and mice. While research use of animals fell from highs in the 1970s, there were almost 4 million 'procedures' begun in 2011. Use of rabbits is on the rise, and more than half of all procedures on rabbits is without use of anaesthetic. See Statistics of Scientific Procedures on Living Animals Great Britain 2011, www.homeoffice.gov.uk. More than 210,000 rabbits were used for research in the United States in 2010: 'US Statistics', www.speakingofresearch.com, accessed 8 September 2012.

29 Charles River commits to a Humane Care Initiative for laboratory animals, but the rabbits are likely not lining up to volunteer for the experiments. 'About Us', www.criver.com, accessed 2 June 2012.

30 Kazutoshi Nishijima, 'Basic Methods for Experimental Rabbits', in *Rabbit Biotechnology: Rabbit Genomics, Transgenesis, Cloning, and Models*, ed. L.-M. Houdebine and J. Fan (Berlin, 2009), pp. 13–33, p. 22.

31 'Rabbit Remix', www.ekac.org, accessed 2 June 2012.

32 'Bunny Center', www.energizer.com, accessed 1 June 2012.

33 'Gift Ideas', www.fitzandfloyd.com, accessed 2 June 2012.

34 'Japan's Bunny Cafes Serve Up Coffee and Cuddles', www.huffingtonpost.com, accessed 2 June 2012.

35 Translated from St John of the Cross, in Daniel James Ladinsky, *Love Poems from God: Twelve Sacred Voices from the East and West* (London, 2002), p. 114.

36 Marinell Harriman, *House Rabbit Handbook: How to Live with an Urban Rabbit* (Alameda, CA, 1991), p. 7.

37 'Hero Rabbit Saves Owners from House Fire', www.reuters.com, 19 September 2011.

A FEW RABBIT POEMS

1 John Kinsella, 'Essay on Myxomatosis', in *The Silo: A Pastoral Symphony* (1995), www.poetrylibrary.edu.au.

2 From E. V. Rieu, *The Flattered Flying Fish and Other Poems* (London, 1962).

3 Lord Alfred Douglas, 'The Rabbit has an evil mind . . .', in A Belgian Hare (pseud.), *Tails with a Twist* (London, 1898).

Select Bibliography

Adams, Richard, *Watership Down* (New York, 1972)

Bement, Caleb N., *The Rabbit Fancier* (New York, 1859)

Brown, Margaret Wise, *The Runaway Bunny* (New York, 1942)

Bunny, Mrs, *Mr and Mrs Bunny – Detectives Extraordinaire!*, translated from *The Rabbit* by Polly Horvath (Toronto, 2012)

Burgess, Thornton W., *The Adventures of Peter Cottontail* (Boston, MA, 1917)

Chapman, Ervin S., *Particeps Criminis: The Story of a California Rabbit Drive* (New York, 1910)

Cheeke, Peter, Nephi M. Patton, Steven D. Lukefahr and James I. McNitt, *Rabbit Production*, 6th edn (Danville, IL, 1987)

Dando-Collins, Stephen, *Pasteur's Gambit: Louis Pasteur, the Australasian Rabbit Plague, and a Ten Million Dollar Prize* (North Sydney, 2008)

Delamer, Eugene, *Pigeons and Rabbits in their Wild: Domestic and Captive States* (London, 1854)

Davis, Susan E., and Margo Demello, *Stories Rabbits Tell: A Natural and Cultural History of a Misunderstood Creature* (New York, 2003)

DiCamillo, Kate, *The Miraculous Journey of Edward Tulane* (Somerville, MA, 2008)

Edwards, R. O., *Rabbits for Exhibition, Pleasure, and Market, Being a Complete Guide for the Amateur and Professional Rabbit Keeper* (London, 1884)

Ezpeleta, Alicia, *Rabbits Everywhere* (New York, 1996)

Garis, Howard R., *Uncle Wiggily Longears; Complete in Two Parts: Fifty-two Stories, One for Each Week of the Year* (New York, 1915)

Harriman, Marinell, *House Rabbit Handbook: How to Live with an Urban Rabbit* (Alameda, CA, 1991)

Harris, Joel Chandler, *Uncle Remus, His Songs and His Sayings: The Folklore of the Old Plantation* (New York, 1881)

Heyward, DuBose, *The Country Bunny and the Little Gold Shoes* (Boston, MA, 1967)

Hodgson, Robert G., *Raising Fur Rabbits* (Toronto, 1927)

Howe, James, and Deborah Howe, *Bunnicula: A Rabbit Tale of Mystery* (New York, 1979)

Jin Yang, *Rabbit: Knowledge of the Twelve Animal Signs and Practices of Chinese Feng-Shui Theory* (n. d.)

Kanable, Anna, *Raising Rabbits* (Emmaus, PA, 1977)

Lebas, F., et al., *The Rabbit: Husbandry, Health and Production*, revd edn (Rome, 1997)

Lloyd Price, R. J., *Rabbits for Profit and Rabbits for Powder: A Treatise on the New Industry of Hutch Farming in the Open, and upon Warrens Specially Intended for Sporting Purposes* (London, 1884)

Lockley, Ronald M., *The Private Life of the Rabbit* (London, 1976)

Lumpkin, Susan, and John Seidensticker, *Rabbits: The Animal Answer Guide* (Baltimore, MD, 2011)

Mougenot, C., and L. Strivay, *Le Pire ami de l'homme: Du lapin de garenne aux guerres biologiques* (Paris, 2011)

Morant, George F., *Rabbits as Food Supply: How to Fold Them on Our Poor Pastures* (London, 1883)

Potter, Beatrix, *The Tale of Peter Rabbit* (London, 1902)

——, *The Tale of Benjamin Bunny* (London, 1904)

——, *The Tale of the Flopsy Bunnies* (London, 1909)

Purchase, Barbara, *The Rabbit and the Hare* (Toronto, 1982)

Riley, Andy, *The Book of Bunny Suicides: Little Fluffy Rabbits Who Just Don't Want to Live Any More* (London, 2003)

——, *Return of the Bunny Suicides* (London, 2004)

Sakai, Stan, *The Art of Usagi Yojimbo* (Milwaukie, OR, 2004)

Seton, Ernest Thompson, *Wild Animals I Have Known* (Toronto, 2006)

Sheail, John, *Rabbits and Their History* (Newton Abbot, 1972)

Stead, D. G., *The Rabbit in Australia* (Sydney, 1935)

Stiteler, Sharon, *Disapproving Rabbits* (New York, 2007)

Thompson, H. V., and C. M. King, *The European Rabbit: The History and Biology of a Successful Colonizer* (Oxford, 1994)

Uttley, Alison, *The Squirrel, The Hare and the Little Grey Rabbit* (London, 1929)

Wallace, Ivy L., *Pookie* (London, 1946)

Williams, C. K., I. Parer, B. J. Coman, J. Burley and M. L. Braysher, *Managing Vertebrate Pests: Rabbits*, Bureau of Resource Sciences/CSIRO Division of Wildlife and Ecology (Canberra, 1995)

Williams, Margery, *The Velveteen Rabbit; or, How Toys Become Real* (London, 1922)

Zolotow, Charlotte, *The Bunny Who Found Easter* (Oakland, CA, 1959)

——, *Mr Rabbit and the Lovely Present* (New York, 1977)

Associations and Websites

AMERICAN RABBIT BREEDERS ASSOCIATION
www.arba.net

ASOCIACIÓN MEXICANA PARA LA CONSERVACIÓN Y ESTUDIO DE LOS
LAGOMORFOS A.C.
www.ibiologia.unam.mx
Mexican Association for the Conservation and Study of Lagomorphs

AUSTRALIAN SHOW RABBIT COUNCIL
www.australianshowrabbitcouncil.com

THE BRITISH RABBIT COUNCIL
www.thebrc.org

THE CANADIAN RABBIT HOPPING CLUB
www.canadianrabbithoppingclub.com

CUNICULTURE INFO
www.cuniculture.info
French website

FÉDÉRATION FRANÇAISE DE CUNICULTURE
www.ffc.asso.fr

FUR AND FEATHER: INCORPORATING RABBITS
www.furandfeather.co.uk
British magazine

HOUSE RABBIT SOCIETY
www.rabbit.org

LAGOMORPH SPECIALIST GROUP
www.ualberta.ca
Run by the International Union for Conservation of Nature (IUCN)
Species Survival Commission

KANIN HOP SCHWEIZ
www.kaninhopschweiz.ch
Rabbit hopping, Switzerland

NIPPON RABBIT CLUB
www.nippon-rabbit-club.com

ORYLAG
www.orylag.com
Website for Orylag rabbit raisers and fur designers

RABBIT ADVOCACY ANIMAL MATTERS
www.rabbitadvocacy.com

RABBIT BREEDERS CANADA
www.rabbitbreeders.ca

THE RABBIT COUNCIL OF NEW ZEALAND (INC.)
www.rabbitcouncil.co.nz

RABBIT WELFARE ASSOCIATION AND FUND, UK
www.rabbitwelfare.co.uk

WORLD LAGOMORPH SOCIETY
www.worldlagomorphsociety.org

WORLD RABBIT SCIENCE ASSOCIATION
www.world-rabbit-science.com
Website of the rabbit industry, responsible for organizing the World
Rabbit Congress

Acknowledgements

I would like to thank our friends and relations who over the years have kept us well supplied with rabbit memorabilia, from the charming to the deeply bizarre. Our children, who have grown up with rabbits, taught us a great deal about the bonds of interspecies affection. Finally, my heartfelt thanks to my parents, who nurtured a love for the small and furred, and to my husband, who has after initial reluctance come to appreciate the comfort of rabbit.

POETRY PERMISSIONS

Elizabeth Coatsworth, 'Song of the Rabbits Outside the Tavern', reproduced by permission of The Marsh Agency Ltd on behalf of the Estate of Elizabeth Coatsworth: p. 103–4; Lord Alfred Douglas, 'The Rabbit has an evil mind . . .', in A Belgian Hare (pseud.), *Tails with a Twist* (London, 1898): p. 183; St John of the Cross, 'A Rabbit Noticed My Condition', from *Love Poems From God, Twelve Sacred Voices from the East and West* by Daniel Ladinsky, copyright © 2002 Daniel Ladinsky and used with his permission: p. 177; 'Essay on Myxomatosis' © John Kinsella and used with his permission, *The Silo* (Fremantle Press, North Fremantle, 1995): pp. 57, 181–2; Emile Victor Rieu, 'The White Rabbit', reproduced by permission of the Authors Licensing & Collecting Society Ltd on behalf of the estate of the late E. V. Rieu: pp. 182–3.

Photo Acknowledgements

Alexander Turnbull Library, Wellington, New Zealand/www.natlib
.govt.nz/ records/22693554: p. 52 (Waite, Keith, 1927–, 'Sensational
Wool Values', *Otago Daily Times*, 16 November 1950, Various Artists:
Collection of Newspaper Clippings, Photocopies and Bromides of
Cartoons by W. Blomfield (A-312-1 and A-312-6), Angus (A-312-2), Paynter
(A-312-3), Tom Scott (A-312-4), W. A. Bowring (A-312-5), Waite (A-312-7)
and Ashley Hunter (A-312-8), Ref: A-312-7-019/by kind permission of R.
K. Waite); Alexander Turnbull Library, Wellington, New Zealand/Royal
New Zealand Returned and Services' Association Collection,
http://mp.natlib.govt.nz/detail/?id=77381: p. 85; Alexander Turnbull
Library, Wellington, New Zealand/www.natlib.govt.nz/records/
22524466: p. 53 ('School Boys Hanging Out Rabbit Skins to Dry, at
Petone', New Zealand Free Lance: Photographic Prints and Negatives,
Ref: PAColl-5936-22); www.ardea.com (M. Watson): p. 25; © The Trustees
of the British Museum: pp. 31, 37, 39, 41, 63, 65, 70, 75, 76, 77, 78, 80, 89,
96, 98, 101, 105, 106, 124, 141, 145, 146, 152; Susan Ford Collins: p. 21;
iStockphoto: pp. 97 (exxorian), 157 (jumaydesigns); morgueFile: pp. 10
(kconnors), 13 (floppy2009), 168 (Kenn W. Kiser); Library of Congress:
pp. 67, 73, 83, 91, 99, 114, 132, 137, 143, 150, 171, 172, 175; National
Archives of Australia: pp. 46 (A13775,2/Barcode 30065202), 49 top
(L16135/Barcode 11305952), 50 (A1200/L44186), 51 (A1200/L44186);
National Library of Australia: p. 44; National Library of Medicine:
p. 170; National Park Service: p. 12 (Dan Johnson); New York Public
Library: p. 113 (Digital ID: 1269161/Record ID: 667915); courtesy of the
People for the Ethical Treatment of Animals, www.peta.org: p. 174; Rex

Features: pp. 6, 17 top (Image Broker), 17 bottom (Richard Austin), 23 (Terry Andrewartha/Nature Picture Library), 55 (Roger-Viollet), 56 (Colin Seddon/Nature Picture Library), 82, 84 top and bottom (Roger-Viollet), 87 (Sipa Press), 92 (Roger-Viollet), 95 (Gérard Lacz), 117 (Everett Collection), 121, 126 (Roger-Viollet), 129 (Royal Mail/Solent News), 138 (Everett Collection), 142 (Associated Newspapers), 158, 162 (Sinopix), 164 (Roger-Viollet), 167 (Action Press), 173 (Sipa Press), 177 (Gary Roberts); Scala Archives: p. 32; Society for Vertebrate Paleontology: p. 8; State Library of Queensland: p. 49 bottom (slq_digitool197791); image courtesy of Documenting the American South, The University of North Carolina at Chapel Hill Libraries: pp. 109, 135; Wisconsin Historical Society, WHS-45276: p. 88.

Index